SACRED MELODIES

FOR

CONFERENCE AND PRAYER MEETINGS,

AND FOR

SOCIAL AND PRIVATE DEVOTION.

"Praise ye the Lord."

TENTH EDITION—REVISED AND AMENDED.

DOVER:
PUBLISHED BY THE FREE-WILL BAPTIST PRINTING ESTABLISHMENT.

WM. BURR, PRINTER.

1851.

HYMNS.

---

1 C. M.

AM I a soldier of the cross,
A follower of the Lamb?
And shall I fear to own his cause,
Or blush to speak his name?

2 Must I be carried to the skies
On flowery beds of ease,
While others fought to win the prize,
And sailed through bloody seas?

3 Are there no foes for me to face?
Must I not stem the flood?
Is this vile world a friend to grace,
To help me on to God?

4 Sure I must fight, if I would reign!
Increase my courage, Lord!
I'll bear the toil, endure the pain,
Supported by thy word.

5 Thy saints in all this glorious war,
Shall conquer, though they die;
They view the triumph from afar
And seize it with their eye.

6 When that illustrious day shall rise,
And all thy armies shine,
In robes of victory through the skies—
The glory shall be thine.

2

C. M.

IN evil long I took delight,
Unawed by shame or fear;
Till a new object struck my sight,
And stopp'd my wild career.

2 I saw one hanging on a tree,
In agonies and blood;
Who fix'd his languid eyes on me,
As near his cross I stood.

3 Sure never to my latest breath
Can I forget that look;
It seemed to charge me with his death,
Though not a word he spoke.

4 My conscience felt and owned the guilt,
And plunged me in despair;
I saw my sins his blood had spilt,
And help'd to nail him there.

5 A second look he gave, which said,
"I freely all forgive;
This blood is for thy ransom paid;
I die, that thou may'st live."

6 Thus while his death my sin displays
In all its blackest hue,
Such are the mysteries of his grace,
It seals a pardon too.

3

L. M.

JESUS my all to heaven has gone,
He whom I fix my hopes upon;
His track I see, and I'll pursue
The narrow way till him I view.

2 The way the holy prophets went,
The road that leads from banishment,
The King's high way of holiness,
I'll go, for all his paths are peace.

3 This is the way I long have sought,
And mourned because I found it not;
My grief a burden long had been,
Because I was not saved from sin.

4 The more I strove against its power,
I felt its weight and guilt the more,
Till late I heard my Savior say,
"Come hither, soul, I am the way!"

5 Lo, glad I come, and thou, blest Lamb,
Shalt take me to thee, as I am:
Nothing but sin have I to give,
Nothing but love shall I receive.

6 Now will I tell to sinners round,
What a dear Savior I have found;
I'll point to thy redeeming blood,
And say, behold the way to God!

4

C. M.

THE rains descended, and the floods
My soul's foundations tried;
While one by one each cherished hope,
Like waning rush-lights died.
And lone and desolate, I heard
The elemental din;
Yet light amid the darkness broke—
A sun-beam shone within.

2 Out on the crested wave I rode,
When the great sea arose,
And challenged with its thunder-cry
The stormy winds as foes.
Then barks were wreck'd, and men went down
Beneath the billowy brine;
But in that tempest of despair,
The sun-beam still was mine.

3 The trust in God, I'll hold it fast,
In peril and in pain,
Until that glorious Sun arise,
Which ne'er shall set again.
O when by death's dim phantom led,
I tread the shadowy vale,
Still shall this perfect peace be mine,
Though flesh and heart should fail.

5

P. M.

HOW precious is the name, brethren sing, brethren sing,
How precious is the name, brethren sing,

How precious is the name of Christ our Paschal Lamb,
Who bore our sin and shame, on the tree, on the tree.

2 I've given all for Christ, he's my all, he's my all,
I've given all for Christ, he's my all;
I've given all for Christ, and my spirit cannot rest,
Unless he's in my breast, reigning there, reigning there.

3 His easy yoke I'll bear, with delight, with delight,
His easy yoke I'll bear, with delight;
His easy yoke I'll bear, and his cross I will not fear,
His name I will declare evermore, evermore.

4 I feel the love of God in my soul, in my soul,
I feel the love of God in my soul;
I feel the love of God, in my heart 'tis shed abroad,
And I will serve my God here below, here below.

6 P. M.

I KNEW I was a sinner, the call it was loud
To repent of my sins, and give up to the Lord;
But O! what distress my soul then was in,
While I was a seeker and yet in my sin!

2 For mercy, for mercy, aloud I did call,
But I could not find mercy till I gave up my all;
And I gave up my all, and the burden did go,
And O! what a love in my heart then did flow.

3 What a bright glowing light in my heart then did shine,
I wonder'd, I wonder'd the Lord was so kind
As to open mine eyes, and give me to see
What a merciful Savior had suffered for me.

4 What joy and what glory then thrilled through my heart,
Which made me quite willing with sinners to part;
And I knew I was willing to let my name go;
And join with the saints in this union below.

5 Come all you poor mourners who feel your distress,
Come, come unto Jesus, and you shall find rest;
The door of salvation is open and free,
Come in now this moment and happy you'll be.

6 There's joy with the angels, there's joy with the saints,
When the news reaches heaven that a sinner repents.
Accept of salvation, no longer delay,
For the voice of Free Grace cries to-day and to-day.

7

C. M.

THIS book is all that's left me now!
Tears will unbidden start;
With falt'ring lip and throbbing brow,
I press it to my heart;
For many generations passed,
Here is our family tree;
My mother's hands this Bible clasped—
She, dying, gave it me.

2 Ah! well do I remember those
Whose names these records bear;
Who round the hearth-stone used to close,
After the evening prayer;
And speak of what these pages said,
In tones my heart would thrill!
Tho' they are with the silent dead,
Here are they living still.

3 My father read this holy book
To brothers, sisters dear—
How calm was my poor mother's look,
Who loved God's word to hear.

Her angel face—I see it yet!
  What thronging memories come!
Again that little group is met,
  Within the walls of home.

4 Thou truest friend man ever knew,
  Thy constancy I've tried;
When all were false I've found thee true,
  My counsellor and guide.
The mines of earth no treasure give,
  That could this volume buy—
In teaching me the way to live,
  It learnt me how to die.

8

I'M a pilgrim, and I'm a stranger,
  I can tarry, I can tarry but a night.
  Do not detain me, for I am going
  To where the streamlets are ever flowing.

2 There the sunbeams are ever shining,
I am longing, I am longing for the sight;
  Within a country unknown and dreary,
  I have been wandering forlorn and weary.

3 Of that country to which I'm going,
My Redeemer, my Redeemer is the light;
  There is no sorrow, or any sighing,
  Or any sinning, or any dying.

9

P. M.

SAW ye my Savior! Saw ye my Savior!
  Saw ye my Savior, the Lord!

O he died on Calvary,
To atone for you and me,
And to purchase our pardon with blood.

2 He was extended, he was extended,
Painfully nail'd to the cross;
There he bow'd his head and died,
There my Lord was crucified,
To atone for a world that was lost.

3 Jesus hung bleeding, Jesus hung bleeding,
Three dreadful hours in pain;
And the solid rocks were rent,
Through creation's vast extent,
When the Jews crucified the dear Lamb.

4 Darkness prevailed, darkness prevailed,
Day was concealed o'er the land;
And the sun refused to shine
While his Majesty divine
Was derided, insulted and slain.

5 When it was finished, when it was finished,
And the atonement was made,
He was taken by the great,
And embalmed in spices sweet,
And was in a new sepulchre laid.

6 Hail mighty Savior, Hail mighty Savior,
Prince and the author of Peace,
Soon he burst the bands of death,
And triumphant, from the earth,
He ascended to mansions of bliss.

7 There interceding, there interceding,
Pleading that sinners may live,
Crying, " See my hands and side,
Father, I was crucified
To redeem them, I pray thee forgive."

8 " I will forgive them, I will forgive them
When they repent and believe;
Let them now return to thee,
And be reconciled to me,
And salvation they all shall receive."

10

8s. & 7s.

NOW behold the Savior pleading,
At the sinner's bolted heart;
Now in heaven he's interceding,
Undertaking sinner's part.

CHORUS.

Sinners, can you hate the Savior?
Will you thrust him from your arms?
Once he died for your behavior—
Now he calls you to his charms.

2 Sinners, hear your God and Savior,
Hear his gracious voice to-day;
Turn from all your vain behavior,
O repent, return and pray.

3 O be wise before you languish
On the bed of dying strife!
Endless joy, or dreadful anguish,
Turn upon the events of life!

4 Now he's waiting to be gracious;
Now he stands and looks on thee,
See what kindness, love and pity,
Shine around on you and me!

5 Open now your hearts before him,
Bid the Savior welcome in;
Now receive, and O, adore him;
Take a full discharge from sin.

6 Come, for all things now are ready;
Yet there's room for many more;
O ye blind, ye lame and needy,
Come to wisdom's boundless store.

11

11s. & 10s.

COME ye disconsolate, where'er you languish,
Come at the mercy seat, fervently kneel;
Here bring your wounded hearts, here tell your anguish;
Earth has no sorrow that Heaven cannot heal.

2 Joy of the comfortless, light of the straying,
Hope when all others die, fadeless and pure;
Here speaks the comforter, in mercy saying,
Earth has no sorrow that Heaven cannot cure.

3 Here see the Bread of Life, see waters flowing
Forth from the throne of God, pure from above;
Come to the feast prepared—come ever knowing,
Earth has no sorrow but Heaven can remove.

12

P. M.

BRETHREN, we have met for worship,
And to adore the Lord our God;
Will you pray with all your power,
While we wait upon the Lord?

All is vain unless the Spirit
Of the Holy one comes down;
Brethren pray, and heavenly manna
Will be showered all around.

2 Don't you see poor sinners round you
Slumbering on the brink of wo?
Death is coming, hell is moving,
Can you bear to let them go?
See your fathers, and your mothers,
And your children sinking down;—
Brethren, pray with all your power,
And the blessing will come down.

3 Don't you see the poor backsliders,
Who were once near heaven's door;
But they've wandered from the Savior,
And are worse than e'er before;
But the Savior offers pardon,
If they will to him return;
Brethren, pray with all your power,
And the blessing will come down.

4 Sisters, will you join and help us,
Moses' sister helped him;
Will you seek the trembling mourners
Who are struggling hard with sin?
Tell them all about the Savior,
Tell them that he will be found;
Sisters, pray with all your power,
And the blessing will come down.

5 Let us love the Lord supremely,
Let us love each other too;

Let us love and pray for sinners,
  Till the Lord creates them new.
Soon he'll call us home to glory,
  At his table we'll sit down;
Christ will gird himself and serve us,
  With sweet manna all around.

13 C. P. M.

WHEN thou my righteous Judge shalt come,
To call thy ransom'd people home,
  Shall I among them stand?
Shall such a worthless worm as I,
Who sometimes am afraid to die,
  Be found at thy right hand?

2 I love to meet among them now,
Before thy gracious throne to bow—
  Though weakest of them all,
And can I bear the piercing thought,
To have my worthless name left out,
  When thou for them shalt call?

3 Prevent, prevent it by thy grace;
Be thou, dear Lord, my hiding place,
  In that expected day.
Thy pard'ning voice, O let me hear,
To still each unbelieving fear,
  Nor let me fall I pray.

4 Among thy saints let me be found,
Whene'er th' Archangel's trump shall sound
  To see thy smiling face:

Then loud through all the crowd I'll sing,
While heav'n's resounding mansions ring,
With shouts of boundless grace.

14 S. M.

DID Christ o'er sinner's weep,
And shall our cheeks be dry?
Let floods of penitential grief
Burst forth from every eye.

2 The Son of God in tears
Angels with wonder see!
Be thou astonish'd, O my soul!
He shed those tears for thee.

3 He wept that we might weep,
Each sin demands a tear;
In heaven alone no sin is found,
And there's no weeping there.

15 P. M.

GLORY to God that I have found
The pearl of my salvation,
We're marching thro' Immanuel's ground,
Up to our heavenly station;
And I'm resolved to follow on,
And never to forsake him,
I'll always keep this narrow way,
Until I overtake him.

2 Fear not, says Christ, ye little flock,
Heirs of immortal glory;
You're built upon the surest rock,
The kingdom lies before you;

Fight on, fight on, ye heirs of grace,
And tell the pleasing story,
I'm always with my little flock,
I'll bring them home to glory.

16 P. M.

DARK and thorny is the desert,
Through which pilgrims make their way,
Yet beyond this vale of sorrow,
Lie the fields of endless day:
Fiends loud howling through the desert
Make them tremble as they go,
And the fiery darts of satan
Often bring their courage low.

2 O young soldier, are you weary
Of the roughness of the way?
Does your strength begin to fail you?
And your vigor to decay?
Jesus, Jesus, will go with you:
He will lead you to his throne;
He who dy'd his garments for you,
And the wine press trod alone.

3 O their crowns, how bright they sparkle,
Such as monarchs never wore:
They have gone to richer pastures,
Jesus is their shepherd there.
Hail! ye happy, happy spirits,
Death no more shall make you fear;
Grief nor sorrow, pain or anguish,
Shall no more distress you there.

17 P. M.

THE pure testimony pour'd forth in the Spirit,
Cuts like a keen two-edged sword;
And hypocrites now are most sorely tormented,
Because they're condemned by the word.
The pure testimony discovers the dross,
While wicked professors make light of the cross;
And Babylon trembles for fear of her loss.

2 Is not the time come for the church to be gather'd
Into the one Spirit of God?
Baptiz'd by one Spirit into the one body,
Partaking Christ's flesh and his blood?
They drink in one spirit which makes them all see
They are one in Christ Jesus, wherever they be,
The Jew and the Gentile, the bond and the free.

3 Then blow ye the trumpet in pure testimony,
And let the world hear it again;
O come ye from Babylon, Egypt and Sodom,
And make your way over the plain;
And gird on your armor, ye saints of the Lord,
For Christ shall direct you by his living word;
The pure testimony will cut like a sword.

4 The great prince of darkness is must'ring his forces,
To make you his pris'ners again,
By flat'ries, reproaches, and vile persecution,
That you in his cause may remain:
But shun his temptations, wherever they lay,
And fear not his servants whatever they say;
The pure testimony will give you the day.

5 The world will not persecute those who are like
them,
But hold them the same as their own;
The pure testimony cries up separation,
And calls you your lives to lay down.
Come out from their spirit and practices too,
The track of the Savior keep still in your view;
The pure testimony will cut the way through.

6 The battle is coming between the two kingdoms,
The armies will gather anon;

The pure testimony and vile persecution
  Will come to close battle ere long:
Then wash all your robes in the blood of the Lamb,
And walk in the spirit as Jesus has done;
In pure testimony you will overcome.

18

11s.

HOW firm a foundation, ye saints of the Lord,
  Is laid for your faith in his excellent word!
What more can he say than to you he hath said,
You who unto Jesus for refuge have fled?

2 In every condition, in sickness and health,
In poverty's vale, or abounding in wealth,
At home or abroad, on the land, on the sea,
'As thy days may demand, shall thy strength ever be.

3 'Fear not, I am with thee, O be not dismayed;
For I am thy God, and will still give thee aid;
I'll strengthen thee, help thee, and cause thee to stand,
Upheld by my righteous omnipotent hand.

4 When through the deep waters I call thee to go,
The rivers of wo shall not thee overflow;
For I will be with thee, thy troubles to bless,
And sanctify to thee thy deepest distress.

5 When through fiery trials thy pathway shall lie,
My grace all sufficient shall be thy supply;
The flame shall not hurt thee; I only design
Thy dross to consume, and thy gold to refine.

6 Even down to old age, all my people shall prove
Impartial, eternal, unchangeable love;
And when hoary hairs shall their temples adorn,
Like lambs they shall still in my bosom be borne.

7 The soul that on Jesus doth lean for repose,
He will not, He will not, desert to his foes;
That soul, tho' all hell should endeavor to shake
He'll never—no never—no never forsake

19

L. M.

WHERE two or three, with sweet accord,
Obedient to their blessed Lord,
Meet to recount his acts of grace:
And offer solemn pray'r and praise,

2 "There," saith the Savior, "will I be,
Amid this little company;
To them unveil my smiling face,
And shed my glory round the place."

3 We meet at thy command, dear Lord,
Relying on thy faithful word;
Now send thy Spirit from above,
And fill our hearts with heavenly love.

20

P. M.

COME, my brethren, let us try,
For a little season;
Every burden to lay by,
Come and let us reason.

2 What is this that casts you down,
What is this that grieves you?
Speak and let the worst be known,
Speaking may relieve you.

3 Think on what your Savior bore,
In the gloomy garden;
Sweating blood from every pore,
Crying, O my Father.

4 See him nailed to the tree,
Bleeding, groaning, dying;

See he suffered this for thee,
Therefore be believing.

5 Joseph took his body down,
Shrouded it in linen;
Laid it in the silent tomb,
And returned mourning.

6 Soon he rises from the tomb,
Angels fly from glory.
O what glory shone around,
Hallelujah, glory.

7 Brethren, don't you feel the flame?
Sisters, dont you love him?
Let us join to praise his name;
Let us never grieve him.

8 Soon we'll meet to part no more,
Soon we'll be in heaven;
There to join with those above,
And forever praise him.

21 P. M.

FROM whence doth this union arise,
That hatred is conquer'd by love?
It fastens our souls in such ties,
That nature and time can't remove.

2 It cannot in Eden be found,
Nor yet in a paradise lost;
It grows on Immanuel's ground,
And Jesus' dear blood it did cost.

3 My friends are so dear unto me,
Our hearts all united in love,
Where Jesus has gone we shall be,
In yonder blest mansion above.

4 Then why so reluctant to part,
Since we shall ere long meet again?
Engraved on Immanuel's heart,
At distance we cannot remain.

5 And when we shall see that bright day,
And join with the angels above,
No longer confined to this clay,
United with Jesus in love:

6 With Jesus we ever shall reign,
And all his bright glory shall see,
And sing, Hallelujah, Amen,
Amen! even so let it be.

22

P. M.

WHITHER goest thou, pilgrim stranger,
Wandering through this lonely vale?
Knowest thou not 'tis full of danger,
And will not thy courage fail?

CHORUS.

No, I'm bound for the kingdom,
Will you go to glory with me?
Hallelujah, O hallelujah,
I'm bound for the kingdom,
Will you go to glory with me,
Hallelujah, praise ye the Lord.

2 Pilgrim thou has justly called me,
Passing through this waste so wide;
But no harm can e'er befall me,
While I'm blessed with such a guide.

3 Such a guide! No guide attends thee,
Hence for thee my fears arise;
If some guardian power befriend thee,
'Tis unseen by human eyes.

4 Yes, unseen, but still believe me,
Such a guide my steps attend;
He'll in every strait relieve me,
He will guide me to the end.

5 Pilgrim, see that stream before thee,
Darkly winding through the vale;
Should its deadly waves roll o'er thee,
Would not then thy courage fail?

6 No, that stream has nothing frightful,
To its brink my steps I'll bend;
Thence to plunge 'twill be delightful,
There my pilgrimage will end.

7 While I gazed, with speed surprising
Down the stream she plunged from sight;
Gazing still I saw her rising,
Like an angel cloth'd with light.

8 Cease my soul, this mourning, crying,
Death will burst the sullen gloom;
Soon my spirit, flutt'ring, flying,
Will be borne beyond the tomb.

23

7s.

BRETHREN, while we sojourn here,
Fight we must but should not fear,
Foes we have, but we've a Friend,
One who loves us to the end;
Forward then with courage go,
Long we shall not dwell below;
Soon the joyful news will come,
Child, your Father calls—come home.

2 In the world a thousand snares,
Lie to take us unawares;
Satan with malicious art,
Watches each unguarded heart;
But from satan's malice free,
Saints shall soon victorious be;
Soon the joyful news will come,
Child, your Father calls—come home.

3 But of all the foes we meet,
None so apt to turn our feet—
None betray us into sin,
Like the foes we have within;
Yet let nothing spoil your peace,
Christ will also conquer these;
Then the joyful news will come,
Child, your Father calls—come home.

24

L. M.

WHEN marshall'd on the nightly plain,
The glittering host bestud the sky,

One star alone of all the train,
Can fix the sinner's wandering eye.

2 Hark! Hark! to God the chorus breaks,
From every host, from every gem;
But one alone the Savior speaks,
It is the star of Bethlehem.

3 Once on the raging seas I rode,
The storm was loud, the night was dark,
The ocean yawn'd and rudely blow'd
The wind that toss'd my foundering bark.

4 Deep horror then my vitals froze,
Death-struck, I ceased the tide to stem;
When suddenly a star arose,
It was the star of Bethlehem.

5 It was my guide, my light, my all,
It bade my dark forebodings cease:
And through the storm and danger's thrall,
It led me to the port of peace.

6 Now safely moor'd, my perils o'er,
I'll sing, first in night's diadem,
Forever and forevermore,
The star—the star of Bethlehem.

25 S. M.

THE day is past and gone;
The evening shades appear;
O may we all remember well,
The night of death draws near.

2 We lay our garments by,
Upon our beds to rest:
So death will soon disrobe us all
Of what we here possess.

3 Lord, keep us safe this night,
Secure from all our fears;
May angels guard us while we sleep,
Till morning light appears.

4 And if we early rise,
And view the unwearied sun,
May we set out to win the prize,
And after glory run.

5 And when our days are past,
And we from time remove,
O may we in thy bosom rest,
The bosom of thy love.

26

11s.

TO leave my dear friends, and with neighbors to part,
And go from my home affects not my heart,
Like the thought of absenting myself for a day
From that blest retreat where I've chosen to pray.

2 Dear bower, where the pine and the poplar have spread,
And woven their branches a roof o'er my head,
How oft have I knelt on the evergreen there,
And poured out my soul to my Savior in prayer.

3 The early shrill notes of a loved nightingale,
That dwelt in my bower I observed as my bell,
To call me to duty, while birds in the air
Sung anthems of praises as I went to prayer.

4 'Twas under the covert of that pleasant grove,
That Jesus my Savior my guilt did remove:
Presented himself as the only true way
Of life and salvation and taught me to pray.

5 How sweet were the zephyrs perfumed with the pine,
The ivy, the balsam, the wild eglantine:
But sweeter, O sweeter, superlative were
The joys that I tasted in answer to prayer.

6 For Jesus my Savior oft deign'd me to meet,
And bless with his presence my humble retreat;
Oft filled me with rapture and blessedness there,
Inditing in heaven's own language my prayer.

7 Dear bower, I must leave you and bid you adieu,
And pay my devotions in parts that are new;
Well knowing my Savior resides every where,
And will in all places give answer to prayer.

27 C. M.

AS on the cross the Savior hung,
And wept and bled and died,
He poured salvation on a wretch,
That languished at his side.

2 His crimes with inward grief and shame,
The penitent confessed;
Then turned his dying eyes to Christ,
And thus his prayer addressed:

3 "Jesus, thou son and heir of heav'n,
Thou spotless Lamb of God!
I see thee bathed in sweat and tears,
And weltering in thy blood.

4 Yet quickly from these scenes of wo,
In triumph thou shalt rise,
Burst through the gloomy shades of death,
And shine above the skies.

5 Amid the glories of that world,
Dear Savior, think on me,
And in the victories of thy death,
Let me a sharer be."

6 His prayer the dying Jesus hears,
And instantly replies,
To-day thy parting soul shalt be
With me in paradise.

28 C. M.

WHAT heavenly music do I hear,
Salvation sounding free;
Ye souls in bondage lend an ear,
This is the Jubilee.

2 How sweetly do the tidings roll,
All round from sea to sea,
From land to land, from pole to pole,
This is the Jubilee.

3 Good news, good news, to Adam's race,
Let Christians all agree
To sing redeeming love and grace,
This is the Jubilee.

4 The gospel sounds a sweet release
To all in misery,
And bids them welcome home to peace,
This is the Jubilee.

5 Jesus is on his mercy seat,
Before him bend the knee;
Let heaven and earth his praise repeat,
This is the Jubilee.

6 Sinners, be wise, return and come,
Unto the Savior flee;
The Spirit bids you welcome home,
This is the Jubilee.

7 Come ye redeemed, your tribute bring,
With songs of harmony;
While on the road to Canaan sing,
This is the Jubilee.

29

8s. & 7s.

COME thou fount of every blessing,
Tune my heart to sing thy grace;
Streams of mercy never ceasing,
Call for songs of loudest praise.

2 Teach me some melodious sonnet,
Sung by flaming tongues above:
Raise the mount, O fix me on it!—
Mount of God's unchanging love.

3 Here I raise my Ebenezer,
Hither by thy help I'm come;
And I hope by thy good pleasure,
Safely to arrive at home.

4 Jesus sought me when a stranger,
Wandering from the fold of God;
He to save my soul from danger,
Interposed his precious blood.

5 Oh! to grace how great a debtor,
Daily I'm constrained to be!
Let thy grace, Lord, like a fetter,
Bind my wandering heart to thee.

6 Prone to wander, Lord, I feel it—
Prone to leave the God I love—
Here's my heart—O take and seal it,
Seal it for thy courts above.

30 S. M.

COME we that love the Lord,
And let our joys be known;
Join in a song of sweet accord,
And thus surround the throne.

2 Let sorrows of the mind
Be banish'd from the place;
Religion never was design'd,
To make our pleasures less.

3 Let those refuse to sing,
Who never knew our God;
But fav'rites of the heavenly King
May speak their joys abroad.

4 The men of grace have found,
Glory begun below,
Celestial fruits on earthly ground,
From faith and hope may grow.

5 The hill of Zion yields
A thousand sacred sweets,
Before we reach the heav'nly fields,
Or walk the golden streets.

6 Then let our songs abound,
  And every tear be dry;
We're marching thro' Immanuel's ground,
  To fairer worlds on high.

31 L. M.

WHEN strangers stand and hear me tell
  What beauties in my Savior dwell;
Where he is gone they fain would know,
That they may seek and love him too.

2 My best beloved keeps his throne
On hills of light in worlds unknown;
But he descends and shows his face,
In the young gardens of his grace.

3 In vineyards planted by his hand,
Where fruitful trees in order stand,
He feeds among the spicy beds,
Where lilies show their spotless heads.

4 He has engross'd my warmest love,
No earthly charms my soul can move;
I have a mansion in his heart,
Nor death nor hell shall make us part.

5 He takes my soul ere I'm aware,
And shows me where his glories are;
Nor ear hath heard, nor tongue can tell
What raptures in his presence dwell.

6 O may my spirit daily rise
On wings of faith above the skies,
Till death shall make my last remove,
To dwell forever with my love.

32

C. M.

SALVATION! O, the joyful sound!
'Tis pleasure to our ears:
A sov'reign balm for every wound,
A cordial for our fears.

2 Buri'd in sorrow and in sin,
At hell's dark door we lay;
But we arise by grace divine
To see a heavenly day.

3 Salvation! let the echo fly
The spacious earth around,
While all the armies of the sky
Conspire to raise the sound.

4 Salvation! O, thou bleeding Lamb,
To thee the praise belongs!
Salvation shall inspire our hearts,
And dwell upon our tongues.

33

H. M.

BY whom was David taught
To aim the dreadful blow,
When he Goliah fought
And laid the Gittite low?
No sword nor spear the stripling took,
But chose a pebble from the brook.

2 'T was Israel's God and King
Who sent him to the fight,
Who gave him strength to sling,
And skill to aim aright.

Ye feeble saints, your strength endures,
Because young David's God is yours.

3 Who ordered Gideon forth
To storm the invader's camp,
With arms of little worth,
A pitcher and a lamp?
The trumpet made his coming known,
And all the host was overthrown.

4 Oh! I have seen the day,
When with a single word,
God helping me to say,
"My trust is in the Lord,"
My soul has quell'd a thousand foes,
Fearless of all that could oppose.

5 But unbelief, self-will,
Self-righteousness and pride,
How often do they steal
My weapons from my side!
Yet David's Lord and Gideon's Friend,
Will help his servant to the end.

34 C. M,

WHEN I can read my title clear,
To mansions in the skies,
I'll bid farewell to every fear,
And wipe my weeping eyes.

2 Should earth against my soul engage,
And hellish darts be hurl'd,
Then I can smile at satan's rage,
And face a frowning world.

3 Let cares like a wild deluge come,
And storms of sorrow fall;
May I but safely reach my home,
My God, my heaven, my all.

4 There shall I bathe my weary soul,
In seas of heavenly rest,
And not a wave of trouble roll,
Across my peaceful breast.

35 C. P. M.

THE Lord into his garden comes;
The spices yield their rich perfumes;
The lilies grow and thrive;
Refreshing showers of grace divine,
From Jesus flow to every vine,
And make the dead revive.

2 This makes the dry and barren ground
In springs of water to abound,
A fruitful soil become!
The desert blossoms as the rose,
When Jesus conquers all his foes,
And makes his people one.

3 The glorious time is rolling on,
The gracious work is now begun,
My soul a witness is;
I taste and see the pardon's free
For all mankind as well as me,
Who comes to Christ may live.

4 The worst of sinners here may find
A Savior pitiful and kind,

Who will them all receive!
None are too late who will repent,
Out of one sinner legions went:
The Lord did him relieve.

5 Come, brethren, ye who love the Lord,
And taste the sweetness of his word,
In Jesus' ways go on;
Our trials and our troubles here,
Will only make us richer there,
When we arrive at home.

6 Amen, Amen, my soul replies,
I'm bound to meet you in the skies,
And claim my mansion there;
Now here's my heart, and here's my hand,
To meet you in that heavenly land,
Where we shall part no more.

36 S. M.

WELCOME sweet day of rest
That saw the Lord arise;
Welcome to this reviving breast,
And these rejoicing eyes!

2 The king himself comes near,
And feasts his saints to-day;
Here we may sit and see him here,
And love, and praise, and pray.

3 One day amid the place,
Where my dear God hath been,
Is sweeter than ten thousand days,
Of pleasurable sin.

4 My willing soul would stay
In such a frame as this,
And sit and sing herself away
To everlasting bliss.

37

L. M. Double.

YOUNG people all attention give,
While I address you in God's name,
You who in sin and folly live,
Come hear the counsel of a friend.
I sought for bliss in glittering toys,
And rang'd th' alluring scenes of life;
But never knew substantial joys,
Till I obeyed my Savior's voice.

2 He spake at once my sins forgiv'n,
And wash'd my load of guilt away;
He gave me glory, peace and heav'n,
And thus I found the heav'nly way.
And now with trembling sense I view,
Huge billows roll beneath your feet,
For death eternal waits for you,
Who slight the force of gospel truth.

3 Youth like the spring will soon be gone,
By rolling years or sudden death;
Your morning sun may set at noon,
And leave you ever in the dark,
Your sparkling eyes and blooming cheeks,
Must wither like the blasted rose;
The coffin, earth and winding sheet,
Will soon your active limbs enclose.

4 O, careless youth, this is the state,
Of all who do free grace refuse;
And soon with you 'twill be too late,
The way of life in Christ to choose.
Come, lay your carnal weapons by;
No longer fight against your God;
But with the gospel now comply,
And heaven shall be your great reward.

38

11s. & 10s.

HAIL thou blest morn, when the great Mediator,
Down from the regions of glory descends;
Shepherds go worship the babe in the manger,
Lo! for his guide the bright angels attend.

CHORUS.

Brightest and best of the sons of the morning,
Shine on our darkness and lend us thine aid;
Star in the east, the horizon adorning,
Guide where our infant Redeemer is laid.

2 Cold on his cradle the dew-drops are shining,
Low lies his bed, with the beasts of the stall;
Angels adore him in slumbers reclining,
Maker, and Monarch, and Savior of all.

3 Say, shall we yield him in costly devotion,
Odors of Eden, and off'rings divine,
Gems of the mountain, and pearls of the ocean,
Myrrh from the forest, and Gold from the mine?

4 Vainly we offer each ample oblation,
Vainly with gold would his favor secure;
Richer by far is the heart's adoration,
Dearer to God are the prayers of the poor.

39

C. M.

COME anxious sinner in whose breast
A thousand thoughts revolve;

Come, with your guilt and fear oppress'd,
And make this last resolve:

2 "I'll go to Jesus, though my sin
Hath like a mountain rose;
I know his courts, I'll enter in,
Whatever may oppose.

3 Prostrate, I'll lie before his throne,
And there my guilt confess;
I'll tell him I'm a wretch undone
Without his pardoning grace.

4 I'll to the gracious King approach,
Whose sceptre pardon gives,
Perhaps he may command me touch,
And then the suppliant lives.

5 Perhaps he will admit my plea,
Perhaps will hear my pray'r;
But if I perish I will pray,
And perish only there.

6 I can but perish if I go;
I am resolved to try:
For if I stay away, I know
I must forever die."

40 P. M.

O HOW happy are they,
Who their Savior obey,
And have laid up their treasures above!
Tongue can never express,
The sweet comfort and peace,
Of a soul in its earliest love.

2 That sweet comfort was mine,
When the favor divine
I first found in the blood of the Lamb—
When my heart first believ'd,
What a joy I receiv'd.
What a heaven in Jesus' dear name!

3 'Twas a heaven below,
My Redeemer to know;
And the angels could do nothing more
Than to fall at his feet,
And the story repeat,
And the lover of sinners adore.

4 Jesus all the day long,
Was my joy and my song;
O that all his salvation might see!
"He hath lov'd me," I cried,
"He hath suffered and died,
To redeem such a rebel as me."

5 On the wings of his love,
I was carried above
All my sins, and temptations, and pain,
And I could not believe
That I ever should grieve,
That I ever should suffer again.

6 O the rapturous height,
Of that holy delight,
Which I felt in the life-giving blood!
Of my Savior possess'd,
I was perfectly blessed,
And was fill'd with the fulness of God.

41

C. M.

I LOVE to steal awhile away
From every cumb'ring care,
And spend the hours of setting day,
In humble, grateful prayer.

2 I love in solitude to shed
The penitential tear,
And all his promises to plead,
Where none but God can hear.

3 I love to think on mercies past,
And future good implore,
And all my care and sorrows cast,
On him whom I adore.

4 I love by faith to take a view
Of brighter scenes in heaven;
The prospect doth my strength renew
While here by tempest driv'n.

5 Thus when life's toilsome day is o'er.
May its departing ray
Be calm as this impressive hour,
And lead to endless day.

42

P. M.

YE objects of sense and enjoyments of time,
Which oft have delighted my heart;
I soon shall exchange you for joys more sublime,
And joys that will never depart.

2 Thou lord of the day and thou queen of the night,
To me ye no longer are known:

I soon shall behold with increasing delight.
A sun that will never go down.

3 Ye wonderful orbs that astonish mine eyes,
Your glories recede from my sight;
I soon shall contemplate more beautiful skies,
And stars more transcendently bright.

4 Ye mountains and valleys, ye rivers and plains,
Thou earth and thou ocean adieu;
More permanent regions where righteousness reigns,
Present their bright hills to my view.

5 My weeping relations, my brethren and friends,
Whose hearts are entwined with my own—
Adieu for the present, my spirit ascends
Where friendship immortal is known.

6 The wrong of transgressors shall grieve me no more,
'Midst foes I no longer reside;
My conflict with sin and with sinners is o'er,
With saints I shall ever abide.

7 No lurking temptation, defilement or fear
Again shall disquiet my breast;
In Jesus' fair image I soon shall appear,
Forever ineffably blest.

8 Ye Sabbaths below which have been my delight,
And now thou blest volume divine;
You've guided my footsteps like stars during night.
Adieu my conductors benign.

9 Thou tottering seat of disease and of pain,
Adieu my dissolving abode;
I soon shall behold and possess thee again,
A beautiful building of God.

10 Come, come, my dear Jesus, come quickly release
The soul thou hast bought with thy blood,
And make me ascend the fair regions of peace,
To feast on the smiles of my God.

43

P. M.

BEGONE unbelief, my Savior is near,
And for my relief, will surely appear:
By prayer let me wrestle, all he will perform,
With Christ in the vessel, I smile at the storm.

2 Though dark be my way, since he is my guide,
'Tis mine to obey, 'tis his to provide;
Though cisterns be broken, and creatures all fail,
The word he hath spoken, will surely prevail.

3 His love in times past forbids me to think,
He'll leave me at last, in trouble to sink.
Each sweet Ebenezer, I have in review,
Confirms his good pleasure to help me quite through.

4 Being willing to save he watched o'er my path,
When Satan's blind slave, I sported with death:
And can he have taught me to trust in his name,
And thus far have brought me, to put me to shame?

5 Why should I complain of want or distress,
Temptations or pain? he told me no less;
The heirs of salvation, I know from his word,
Through much tribulation must follow their Lord.

6 How bitter that cup, no heart can conceive,
Which he drank quite up that sinners might live!
His way was much rougher and darker than mine,
Did Jesus thus suffer, and shall I repine?

7 Since all that I meet shall work for my good,
The bitter is sweet, the med'cine is food:
Tho' painful at present, 'twill cease before long,
And then, oh how pleasant the conqueror's song.

44

7s. & 6s.

O WHEN shall I see Jesus,
And reign with him above,
And from that flowing fountain
Drink everlasting love!

When shall I be delivered
From this vain world of sin,
And with my blessed Jesus
Drink endless pleasures in ?

2 But now I am a soldier,
My Captain's gone before;
He's given me my orders,
And bid me not give o'er.
If I continue faithful,
A righteous crown he'll give,
And all his valiant soldiers
Eternal life shall have.

3 Through grace I am determined
To conquer though I die;
And then away to Jesus
On wings of love I'll fly.
Farewell to sin and sorrow,
I bid you all adieu;
And O, my friends, be faithful,
And on your way pursue.

4 And if you meet with troubles
And trials on your way,
Then cast your cares on Jesus,
And don't forget to pray;
Gird on the heavenly armor
Of faith and hope and love,
And when the combat's ended,
He'll carry you above.

5 O do not be discourag'd,
For Jesus is your friend;

And if you want more knowledge,
He'll not refuse to lend;
Neither will he upbraid you,
Though often you request;
He'll give you grace to conquer,
And take you home to rest.

6 And when the last loud trumpet
Shall rend the vaulted skies,
And bid the entombed millions
From their cold beds arise,
Our ransom'd dust revived,
Bright beauties shall put on,
And soar to the blest mansions
Where our Redeemer 's gone.

45

11s.

A FOUNTAIN in Jesus which runs always free,
For washing and cleansing such sinners as we;
Our sins, though like crimson, made white as the wool,
No lack in the fountain, it always is full.

2 All things now are ready, he invites us to come,
The supper is made by the Father and Son;
Rich bounties, rich dainties, here we may receive,
A living forever, if we will believe.

3 The guests who were bidden, refused the call;
For they were not ready nor willing at all,
To be stripped of their honor, and part with their store,
For a feast that was given and made for the poor.

4 If they are not ready, and wish to delay,
My house shall be filled, the Father doth say;
The highways and hedges, the halt and the blind,
Shall come and be welcome, the supper is mine.

5 He decks us with jewels, and rings of rich kind;
A garment not woven, but richly refin'd;
Redeemed by Jesus, made heirs with the King,
A plan of the Father in glory to sing.

46

8s., 7s. & 4s.

LO! he comes, with clouds descending,
Once for favor'd sinners slain!
Thousand, thousand saints attending,
Swell the triumph of his train:
Hallelujah!
Jesus comes—and comes to reign.

2 Every eye shall now behold him,
Robed in dreadful majesty!
Those who set at nought and sold him,
Pierced and nail'd him to the tree,
Deeply wailing,
Shall the true Messiah see!

3 When the solemn trump has sounded,
Heaven and earth shall flee away;
All who hate him must, confounded,
Hear the summons of that day—
'Come to judgment!—
Come to judgment!—come away!'

4 Yea, amen!—let all adore thee,
High on thine eternal throne!
Savior, take the power and glory:
Make thy righteous sentence known!
Oh, come quickly—
Claim the kingdom for thine own!

47

L. M. WITH CHORUS.

THE Gospel trumpet has been blown,
And caused poor sinners to return
To Jesus Christ our heavenly king,
To join and shout and praise and sing.
For we're on our march for glory,
We will sing salvation free;
Yes, we are on our march to glory,
Let us sound the Jubilee.

2 If we prove faithful to the end,
We find in Christ a glorious Friend,
For he who guards us, watches, keeps,
He never slumbers, never sleeps,
For the Lord is in the desert,
He is on the land and sea;
Yes, the Lord is in the desert,
Let us sound the Jubilee.

3 May we obey the gracious call,
Of him whose love extends to all;
He's never weary, never faint,
He hears and pities each complaint.
For he knows our heart's desires
When we bend the humble knee;
Yes, he wipes away our tears,
And he gives us victory.

4 When on the part of God we rise,
We take the cross and win the prize;
So when the evening shades prevail,
Our songs of triumph shall not fail.

Now we're on our way to heaven,
We will sing salvation free;
Yes, we're on our way to heaven,
We will sound the Jubilee.

5 And when our pilgrimage is o'er,
On wings of triumph may we soar,
Where floods of glory ceaseless roll,
Where beauties charm our precious souls.
There we'll join in singing praises,
To Immanuel our King;
There we'll join in shouting glory,
Till we make the arches ring.

6 The gospel heralds have gone forth,
To spread glad tidings through the earth,
From east to west they shall proclaim
Salvation through the Savior's name.
For the Spirit is out-pouring,
On the land and on the sea;
Yes, the Spirit is out-pouring,
Let us sound the Jubilee.

48 C. M.

JERUSALEM, my happy home,
O how I long for thee!
When will my sorrows have an end?
Thy joys, when shall I see?

2 Thy walls are all of precious stone,
Most glorious to behold;
Thy gates are richly set with pearl,
Thy streets are paved with gold.

3 Thy garden and thy pleasant walks,
   My study long have been ;
Such dazzling views by human sight,
   Have never yet been seen.

4 If heaven be thus so glorious Lord,
   Why should I stay from thence ?
What folly's this that I should dread
   To die and go from hence ?

5 Reach down, O Lord, thine arm of grace,
   And cause me to ascend,
Where congregations ne'er break up,
   And Sabbaths never end.

6 When we've been there ten thousand years,
   Bright shining as the sun,
We've no less days to sing God's praise,
   Than when we first begun.

49

7s.

HARK! my soul, it is the Lord,
'Tis thy Savior, hear his word ;
Jesus speaks, he speaks to thee,
Say, poor sinner, " Lovest thou me ?"

2 " I delivered thee when bound,
And when bleeding, heal'd thy wound,
Sought thee wand'ring, set thee right,
Turned thy darkness into light.

3 " Can a mother's tender care,
Cease toward the child she bear ?

Yes! she may forgetful be,
Yet will I remember thee.

4 "Mine is an unchanging love,
Higher than the heights above,
Deeper than the depths beneath,
Free and faithful, strong as death.

5 "Thou shalt see my glory soon,
When the work of faith is done,—
Partner of my throne shalt be,
Say, poor sinner, lovest thou me?"

6 Lord, it is my chief complaint,
That my love is still so faint;
Yet I love thee and adore;—
O for grace to love thee more!

50

8s., 7s. & 4s.

SINNERS, will you scorn the message,
Sent in mercy from above?
Every sentence—O how tender!
Every line is full of love;
Listen to it—
Every line is full of love.

2 Hear the heralds of the Gospel
News from Zion's King proclaim,
To each rebel sinner—"Pardon,
Free forgiveness in his name."
How important!
Free forgiveness in his name.

3 Tempted souls, they bring you succor;
Fearful hearts, they quell your fears;
And with news of consolation,
Chase away the falling tears:
Tender heralds—
Chase away the falling tears.

4 False professors, grovelling worldlings,
Callous hearers of the word,
While the messengers address you,
Take the warnings they afford;
We entreat you,
Take the warnings they afford.

5 Who hath our report believed?
Who received the joyful word?
Who embrac'd the news of pardon,
Offer'd to you by the Lord?
Can you slight it—
Offer'd to you by the Lord!

6 O, ye angels, hovering round us,
Waiting spirits, speed your way,
Hasten to the court of heaven,
Tidings bear without delay:
Rebel sinners,
Glad the message will obey.

51 C. M.

COME Holy Spirit, heav'nly dove,
With all thy quick'ning pow'rs—
Kindle a flame of sacred love
In these cold hearts of ours.

2 In vain we tune our formal songs
In vain we strive to rise;
Hosannas languish on our tongues,
And our devotion dies.

3 Dear Lord! and shall we ever live
At this poor dying rate?
Our love so faint, so cold to thee,
And thine to us so great?

4 Come, Holy Spirit, heav'nly dove,
With all thy quick'ning pow'rs,—
Come, shed abroad a Savior's love,
And that shall kindle ours.

52 C. M.

O FOR a closer walk with God,
A calm and heavenly frame;
A light to shine upon the road
That leads me to the Lamb?

2 Where is the blessedness I knew
When first I saw the Lord?
Where is the soul-refreshing view
Of Jesus and his word?

3 What peaceful hours I then enjoyed?
How sweet their memory still!
But now I find an aching void
The world can never fill.

4 Return, O holy dove! return
Sweet messenger of rest!

I hate the sins that made thee mourn,
And drove thee from my breast.

5 The dearest idol I have known,
Whate'er that idol be,
Help me to tear it from thy throne,
And worship only thee.

6 So shall my walk be close with God,
Calm and serene my frame;
So, purer light shall mark the road
That leads me to the Lamb.

53 C. M.

ALAS! and did my Savior bleed?
And did my Sovereign die!
Would he devote that sacred head
For such a worm as I?

2 Thy body slain, sweet Jesus, thine,
And bath'd in its own blood,
While all exposed to wrath divine,
The glorious sufferer stood!

3 Was it for crimes that I had done,
He groaned upon the tree?
Amazing pity, grace unknown!
And love beyond degree!

4 Well might the sun in darkness hide,
And shut his glories in,
When Christ, the mighty Savior, died,
For man, the creature's sin.

5 Thus might I hide my blushing face,
While his dear cross appears,
Dissolve my heart in thankfulness,
And melt my eyes in tears.

6 But drops of grief can ne'er repay
The debt of love I owe:
Here, Lord, I give myself away;
'Tis all that I can do.

54 H. M.

ARISE, my soul, arise,
Shake off thy guilty fears,
The bleeding sacrifice
In my behalf appears;
Before the throne my surety stands,
My name is written on his hands.

2 He ever lives above,
For me to intercede,
His all redeeming love,—
His precious blood to plead;
His blood atoned for all our race,
And sprinkles now the throne of grace.

3 Five bleeding wounds he bears,
Receiv'd on Calvary,
They pour effectual prayers,
They strongly speak for me:
Forgive him, O forgive, they cry,
Nor let that ransomed sinner die.

4 The Father hears him pray,
His dear anointed one;

He cannot turn away
The presence of his Son;
His spirit answers to the blood,
And tells me I am born of God.

5 My God is reconcil'd,
His pardoning voice, I hear;
He owns me for his child,
I can no longer fear;
With confidence I now draw nigh,
And Father, Abba Father, cry.

55

11s.

O TURN ye, poor sinners, for why will ye die,
When God, in great mercy, is coming so nigh,
Now Jesus invites, and the Spirit says come,
And angels are waiting to welcome you home.

2 How vain the delusion that while you delay,
Your hearts may grow better by staying away!
Come wretched, come starving, come just as you be,
While streams of salvation are flowing so free.

3 And now Christ is ready your souls to receive,
O, how can you question, if you will believe?
If sin is your burden, why will you not come?
'Tis you he bids welcome; he bids you come home.

4 In riches, in pleasure, what can you obtain
To soothe your affliction, or banish your pain?
To bear up your spirit when summoned to die,
Or waft you to mansions of glory on high?

5 Why will you be starving or feeding on air?
There's mercy in Jesus, enough and to spare;
If still you are doubting, make trial and see,
And prove that his mercy is boundless and free.

6 Come give us your hand, and the Savior your heart,
And trusting in heaven we never shall part:

O how can we leave you? why will you not come?
We'll journey together, and soon be at home.

56

8s. & 7s.

JESUS, I my cross have taken,
All to leave and follow thee;
Naked, poor, despised, forsaken,
Thou from hence my all shalt be:
Perish every fond ambition,
All I've sought, or hoped, or known:
Yet how rich is my condition!
God and heaven are all my own.

2 Let the world despise and leave me—
They have left my Savior too;
Human hearts and looks deceive me,
Thou art not, like them, untrue:
And whilst thou shalt smile upon me,
God of wisdom, love, and might,
Foes may hate and friends disown me,
Show thy face and all is bright.

3 Go then, earthly fame and treasure;
Come disaster, scorn and pain;
In thy service pain is pleasure,
With thy favor loss is gain;
I have called thee, Abba Father,
I have set my heart on thee;
Storms may howl, and clouds may gather,
All must work for good to me.

4 Man may trouble and distress me,
'T will but drive me to thy breast;

Life with trials hard may press me,
  Heaven will bring me sweeter rest:
Oh! 'tis not in grief to harm me,
  While thy love is left to me;
Oh! 't were not in joy to charm me,
  Were that joy unmixed with thee.

5 Haste thee on, from grace to glory,
  Armed by faith and winged by prayer:
Heaven's eternal day 's before thee,
  God's own hand shall guide thee there:
Soon shall close thy earthly mission,
  Soon shall pass thy pilgrim days;
Hope shall change to glad fruition,
  Faith to sight, and prayer to praise.

57 C. P. M.

MY days, my weeks, my months, my years,
Fly rapid as the whirling spheres
  Around the steady pole;
Time like the tide its motion keeps,
And I must launch through boundless deeps,
  Where endless ages roll.

2 The grave is near the cradle seen,
How swift the moments pass between,
  And whisper as they fly:
"Unthinking man, remember this,
Though fond of sublunary bliss,
  That you must groan and die."

3 How great the bliss, how great the wo
Hangs on this inch of time below,

On this precarious breath!
The Lord of nature only knows,
Whether another year shall close,
Ere I expire in death.

4 But will my soul be then extinct,
And cease to live, and cease to think?
It cannot, cannot be;
No, my immortal cannot die;
What wilt thou do, or whither fly,
When death shall set thee free?

5 Will mercy then her arms extend,
Will Jesus be thy guardian friend?
And heaven thy dwelling place?
Or shall insulting fiends appear,
To drag thee down to dark despair,
Below the reach of grace?

6 A heaven or hell, and these alone,
Beyond the present life are known,
There is no middle state;
To-day attend the call divine,
To-morrow may be none of thine,
Or it may be too late.

58

8s.

HOW tedious and tasteless the hours,
When Jesus no longer I see,
Sweet prospects, sweet birds, and sweet flowers,
Have lost all their sweetness to me.

The midsummer sun shines but dim;
The fields strive in vain to look gay;
But when I am happy in him,
December's as pleasant as May.

2 His name yields the richest perfume,
And sweeter than music his voice,
His presence disperses my gloom,
And makes all within me rejoice.
I should, were he always thus nigh,
Have nothing to wish or to fear,
No mortal so happy as I;
My summer would last all the year.

3 Content with beholding his face,
My all to his pleasure resign'd,
No changes of season or place,
Would make any change in my mind;
While blest with a sense of his love,
A palace a toy would appear,
And prisons would palaces prove,
If Jesus would dwell with me there.

4 Dear Lord, if indeed I am thine,
If thou art my sun and my song,
Say why do I languish and pine,
And why are my winters so long?
O drive these dark clouds from my sky,
Thy soul-cheering presence restore,
O take me to thee upon high,
Where winter and clouds are no more.

59 L. M.

O COULD my soul this morning rise,
And feel that life that never dies;

I'd praise that hand with all my powers,
That guarded my unguarded hours.

2 'Tis he who gives me life divine,
In him eternal joys are mine;
Then rouse, my soul, bid sloth adieu,
Thy Jesus love and him pursue.

3 Haste on to that immortal shore,
Where night and sleep are known no more;
There shall I soon in glory rise,
With seraphs in a sweet surprise.

4 Then shall I raise a morning song,
With all the vast angelic throng;
Singing in everlasting peace,
My morning song shall never cease.

60 C. P. M.

HOW happy is the pilgrim's lot,
How free from every anxious thought,
From worldly hope and fear!
Confin'd to neither court nor cell,
His soul disdains on earth to dwell;
He only sojourns here.

2 This happiness in part is mine;
Already sav'd from low design,—
From every creature-love—
Bless'd with the scorn of finite good,
My soul is lightened of its load,
And seeks the things above.

3 The things eternal I pursue,
And happiness beyond the view
Of those who basely pant
For things by nature felt and seen,
Their honors, wealth, and pleasures mean,
I neither have nor want.

4 Nothing on earth I call my own:
A stranger to the world unknown,
I all their goods despise;
I trample on their whole delight,
And seek a city out of sight,—
A city in the skies.

5 There is my house and portion fair;
My treasure and my heart are there,
And my abiding home;
For me my elder brethren stay,
And angels beckon me away,
And Jesus bids me come.

61

P. M.

O THOU in whose presence
My soul takes delight,
On whom in affliction I call;
My comfort by day,
And my song in the night,
My hope, my salvation and all.

2 Where dost thou at noon-tide
Resort with thy sheep,
To feed in the pastures of love ?

For why in the valley
Of death should I weep,
Or alone in the wilderness rove?

3 O why should I wander
An alien from thee—
Or cry in the desert for bread?
Thy foes will rejoice,
When my sorrow they see,
And smile at the tears I have shed.

4 Ye daughters of Zion,
Declare have you seen
The star that on Israel shone.
Say, if in your tents
My beloved has been,
Or where with his flock he has gone.

5 This is my beloved,
His form is divine,
His vestments shed odors around:
The locks of his head
Are as grapes on the vine,
When autumn with plenty is crown'd.

6 Like the fair rose of Sharon,
Or lilies that grow
In the vales, on the banks of the streams,
On his cheeks does the beauty
Of excellence glow,
And his eyes as the sun's radiant beams.

7 His voice as the sound
Of the dulcimer sweet,
Is heard through the shadow of death;

The cedars of Lebanon
Bow at his feet,
And the air is perfumed with his breath.

8 His lips as a fountain
Of righteousness flow,
That waters the garden of grace.
From thence, their salvation,
The Gentiles shall know,
And bask in the smiles of his face.

9 Love sits on his eyelids,
And scatters delight,
Through all the bright mansions on high;
Their faces the cherubim
Veil in his sight,
And praise him with fullness of joy.

10 He looks, and ten thousands
Of angels rejoice,
And myriads wait for his word!
He speaks, and eternity,
Fill'd with his voice,
Re-echoes the praise of the Lord.

62 C. M.

ON Jordan's stormy banks I stand,
And cast a wishful eye,
To Canaan's fair and happy land,
Where my possessions lie.

2 O the transporting rapt'rous scene,
That rises to my sight!

Sweet fields arrayed in living green.
And rivers of delight.

3 There gen'rous fruits that never fail,
On trees immortal grow;
There rocks and hills, and brooks and vale,
With milk and honey flow.

4 All o'er those wide extended plains,
Shines one eternal day;
There God the Son forever reigns,
And scatters night away.

5 No chilling winds nor pois'nous breath,
Can reach that healthful shore;
Sickness and sorrow, pain and death,
Are felt and feared no more.

6 When shall I reach that happy place,
And be forever blest,
When shall I see my Father's face,
And in his bosom rest?

7 Fill'd with delight, my raptur'd soul,
Would here no longer stay!
Though Jordan's waves around me roll,
Fearless I'd launch away.

8 There on those high and flowery plains,
Our spirits ne'er shall tire;
But in perpetual joyful strains,
Redeeming love admire.

63 C. M.

LORD, at thy temple we appear,
As happy Simeon came,

And hope to meet our Savior here;
O, make our joys the same.

2 With what divine and vast delight,
The good old man was fill'd,
When fondly in his wither'd arms,
He clasped the holy child.

3 Now I can leave this world, he cried,
Behold thy servant dies!
I've seen thy great salvation, Lord,
And close my peaceful eyes.

4 This is the light prepared to shine,
Upon the Gentile lands:
Thine Israel's glory, and their hope,
To break their slavish bands.

5 Jesus! the vision of thy face,
Hath overpowering charms,
Scarce shall I feel death's cold embrace,
If Christ be in my arms.

6 Then while ye hear my heart-strings break,
How sweet my minutes roll!
A mortal paleness on my cheek,
And glory in my soul.

64 P. M.

THERE is an hour of peaceful rest,
To mourning wand'rers given,
There is a joy for souls distrest,
A balm for every wounded breast,
'Tis found above in heaven.

2 There is a soft, a downy bed,
'Tis fair as breath of even,
A couch for weary mortals spread,
Where they may rest the aching head,
And find repose in heaven.

3 There is a home for weary souls,
By sin and sorrow driven,
When tossed on life's tempestuous shoals,
Where storms arise and ocean rolls,
And all is drear—but heaven.

4 Now faith lifts up the tearless eye,
To brighter prospects given;
And views the tempest passing by,
Sees evening shadows quickly fly,
And all serene in heaven.

5 There fragrant flowers immortal bloom,
And joys supreme are given,
There rays divine disperse the gloom;
Beyond the dark and narrow tomb,
Appears the dawn of heaven.

65

L. M.

HE dies! the Friend of sinners dies,
Lo! Salem's daughters weep around!
A solemn darkness veils the skies!
A sudden trembling shakes the ground.

2 Come, saints, and drop a tear or two,
For him who groaned beneath your load;
He shed a thousand drops for you—
A thousand drops of richer blood.

3 Here's love and grief beyond degree—
  The Lord of glory dies for men!
But lo! what sudden joys we see!
  Jesus, the dead—revives again!

4 The rising Lord forsakes the tomb!
  (In vain the tomb forbids his rise,)
Cherubic legions guard him home,
  And shout him welcome to the skies.

5 Break off your tears, ye saints, and tell,
  How high your great Deliverer reigns,
Sing how he spoiled the hosts of hell,
  And led the tyrant death in chains!

6 Say, "Live forever, glorious King,
  Born to redeem, and strong to save!"
Then ask—"O death, where is thy sting?
  And where thy vict'ry, boasting grave!"

66

O COME, come away from sin, that dreadful monster—
Let Christ awhile, upon you smile,
  O come, come away;
O come and test redeeming love,
And then his truth will friendship prove,
And onward sweetly move,—
  O come, come away.

From death and the curse in which you now are sinking,
Redeeming love will you remove,
  O come, come away;

O come along, and join our throng,
And with us sing our cheerful song,
And heaven shall be your home—
O come, come away.

While watchmen are standing on the walls of Zion,
Inviting you to join them too,
O come, come away;
O will you still refuse the call,
And into misery blindly fall,
And drink down the burning gall —
O come, come away.

When freed from this world of sorrow and temptation,
We'll sail above, on wings of love,
O come, come away;
And with angelic armies sing,
And make the heavenly arches ring,
We'll praise our eternal king,—
O come, come away.

The bright morn of youth will soon be gone forever;
Its morning light will set at night,
O come, come away;
O come while youth is in its prime,
And seek Redeeming love divine,
And in Christ's army shine,—
O come, come away.

67 C. M.

HOW happy every child of grace,
Who knows his sins forgiven;

This earth, he cries, is not my place,
I seek my place in heaven :
A country far from mortal sight,—
Yet, O! by faith I see
The land of rest, the saint's delight,
The heaven prepared for me.

2 O what a blessed hope is ours,
While here on earth we stay,
We more than taste the heavenly powers,
And antedate that day;
We feel the resurrection near,
Our life in Christ concealed,
And with his glorious presence here,
Our earthen vessels filled.

3 O, would he more of heaven bestow,
And let the vessels break;
And let our ransom'd spirits go,
To grasp the God we seek?
In rapturous awe, on him to gaze,
Who bought the sight for me;
And shout and wonder at his grace,
To all eternity.

68

8s. 7s. & 4s.

COME, ye sinners, poor and needy,
Weak and wounded, sick and sore,
Jesus ready stands to save you,
Full of pity, love and power;
He is able,
He is willing, doubt no more.

2 Now, ye needy, come and welcome,
God's free bounty glorify;
True belief and true repentance,
Every grace that brings you nigh,
Without money,
Come to Jesus Christ and buy.

3 Let not conscience make you linger,
Nor of fitness fondly dream;
All the fitness he requireth
Is to feel your need of him:
This he gives you,
'Tis the spirit's glimm'ring beam.

4 Come ye weary, heavy-laden,
Bruis'd and mangled by the fall,
If you tarry till you're better,
You will never come at all:
Not the righteous,—
Sinners, Jesus came to call.

5 Agonizing in the garden,
Lo! your Maker prostrate lies;
On the bloody tree behold him!
Hear him cry before he dies,
"It is finished!"
Sinners, will not this suffice?

6 Lo! th' incarnate God ascending,
Pleads the merit of his blood;
Venture on him, venture freely;
Let no other trust intrude;
None but Jesus
Can do helpless sinners good.

7 Saints and angels joined in concert,
Sing the praises of the Lamb,
While the blissful seats of heaven,
Sweetly echo with his name;
Hallelujah!
Sinners here may do the same.

69

11s.

WHY sleep we, my brethren, come let us arise,
O, why should we slumber in sight of the prize?
Salvation is nearer, our days are far spent,
O, let us be active—awake! and repent.

2 O, how can we slumber! the Master is come,
And calling on sinners to seek them a home;
The Spirit and Bride now in concert unite,
The weary they welcome, the careless invite.

3 O, how can we slumber! our foes are awake;
To ruin poor souls, every effort they make,
To accomplish their object, no means are untried,
The careless they comfort, the wakeful misguide.

4 O, how can we slumber! when so much was done,
To purchase salvation, by Jesus, the Son!
Now mercy is proffer'd, and justice display'd,
Now God can be honored and sinners be sav'd.

5 O, how can we slumber! when death is so near,
And sinners are sinking to endless despair;
Now prayers may avail, and they gain the high prize,
Before they in torment shall lift up their eyes.

6 O, how can we slumber! ye sinners look round,
Before the last trumpet your hearts shall confound;
O, fly to the Savior, he calls you to-day;
While mercy is waiting, O make no delay.

70

11s. WITH CHORUS.

THE pleasures of earth, I have seen fade away,
They bloom for a season, but soon they decay,
But pleasures more lasting in Jesus are given,
Salvation on earth, and a mansion in heaven.
Home, home, sweet, sweet home,
The saints in those mansions are ever at home.

2 Allure me no longer, ye false glowing charms!
The Savior invites me, I'll go to his arms;
At the banquet of mercy I hear there is room,
O there may I feast with his children at home.
Home, home, sweet, sweet home,
O Jesus, conduct me to heaven, my home.

3 Farewell, vain amusements, my follies adieu,
While Jesus and heaven and glory I view;
I feast on the pleasures that flow from his throne,
The foretaste of heaven, sweet heaven, my home.
Home, home, sweet, sweet home,
O when shall I share the fruition of home?

4 The days of my exile are passing away,
The time is approaching, when Jesus will say,
"Well done, faithful servant, sit down on my throne,
And dwell in my presence forever at home."
Home, home, sweet, sweet home,
O there shall I rest with the Savior at home.

5 Affliction and sorrow and death shall be o'er,
The saints shall unite to be parted no more;
Then loud hallelujahs fill heaven's high dome,
They dwell with the Savior forever at home.
Home, home, sweet, sweet home,
They dwell with the Savior, forever at home.

71

C. M.

I'M not ashamed to own my Lord,
Nor to defend his cause;

Maintain the honor of his word,
The glory of his cross.

2 Jesus, my God! I know his name,
His name is all my trust;
Nor will he put my soul to shame,
Or let my hope be lost.

3 Firm as his throne, his promise stands;
And he can well secure
What I've committed to his hands,
Till the decisive hour.

4 Then will he own my worthless name
Before his Father's face,
And in the New Jerusalem
Appoint my soul a place.

72 11s.

I WOULD not live alway, I ask not to stay
Where storm after storm rises o'er the dark way;
The few lurid mornings that dawn on us here,
Are enough for life's woes—full enough for its cheer.

2 I would not live alway, no—welcome the tomb,
Since Jesus has lain there, I dread not its gloom;
There, sweet be my rest, till he bid me arise,
To hail him in triumph descending the skies.

3 Who, who would live alway, away from his God;
Away from yon heaven, that blissful abode,
Where rivers of pleasure flow o'er the bright plains,
And the noon-tide of glory eternally reigns.

4 Where saints of all ages in harmony meet,
Their Savior and brethren, transported to greet,
While anthems of rapture unceasingly roll,
And the smile of the Lord is the feast of the soul.

73

S. M.

AH, whither should I go,
Burdened, and sick and faint?
To whom should I my trouble show,
And pour out my complaint?

2 My Savior bids me come;
Ah! why do I delay?
He calls the weary sinner home,
And yet from him I stray!

3 What is it keeps me back
From which I cannot part?
Which will not let the Savior take
Possession of my heart?

4 Some cursed thing unknown,
Must surely lurk within:
Some idol which I will not own;
Some secret bosom sin.

5 Jesus, the hind'rance show,
Which I have feared to see;
And let me now consent to know
What keeps me back from thee.

6 Searcher of hearts,—in mine
Thy trying power display;
Into its darkest corners shine,
And take the veil away.

74

C. M.

ALMIGHTY Savior, here we stand,
Ranged by the water side;

Hither we come at thy command,
To wait upon thy bride.

2 Thy footsteps marked this humble way,
For all that love thy cause;
Lord! thy example we obey,
And glory in the cross.

3 Our dearest Lord, we'll follow thee,
Wher'er thou lead'st the way;
Thro' floods, thro' flames, thro' death's dark
vale,
To realms of endless day.

75 C. P. M.

SALEM'S bright King, Jesus by name,
In ancient time to Jordan came,
All righteousness to fill;
'T was there the ancient Baptist stood,
Whose name was John, a man of God,
To do his Master's will.

2 The Holy Jesus did demand
His right to be baptized, and then
The Baptist gave consent:
On Jordan's banks they did prepare,
The Baptist and his Master dear,
Then down the bank they went.

3 Down in old Jordan's rolling stream,
The Baptist led the holy Lamb,
And there did him baptize;

Jehovah saw his darling Son,
And was well pleas'd in what he'd done,
And owned him from the skies.

4 The opening heaven now complies,
The Holy Ghost like lightning flies,
Down from the courts above;
And on the holy, heavenly Lamb,
The spirit lights and does remain,
In shape like a fair dove.

5 "This is my Son," Jehovah cries,
The echoing voice from glory flies,
"O children, hear ye him;"
Hark! 'tis his voice, behold! he cries,
"Repent, believe and be baptized,
And wash away your sins."

6 Come, children, come, his voice obey,
Salem's bright King has mark'd the way,
And has a crown prepar'd.
O, then arise and give consent,
Walk in the way that Jesus went,
And have the great reward.

7 Believing children, gather round,
And let your joyful songs abound,
With cheerful hearts arise:
See, here is water, here is room,
A loving Savior, calling, "Come,
O children, be baptiz'd."

8 Behold! his servant waiting stands,
With willing heart and ready hands,
To wait upon the bride;

Ye candidates, your hearts prepare,
And let us join in solemn prayer,
Down by the water side.

76 L. M.

DO we not know that solemn word,
That we are buried with the Lord?
Baptized into his death, and then
Put off the body of our sin?

2 Our souls receive diviner breath,
Raised from corruption, guilt, and death;
So from the grave did Christ arise,
And lives to God above the skies.

3 No more let sin or Satan reign
Over our mortal flesh again;
The various lusts, we served before,
Shall have dominion now no more.

77 8s. 7s. & 4s.

TO the flowing stream of Jordan,
Lo! the King of Zion came;
There the ancient Baptist waited,
To immerse the spotless Lamb;
They descended,
To the Savior's watery grave.

2 Come then ye who love the Savior,
Fear ye not to own your Lord,
Reckless if the world should scorn you,
Follow Christ, obey his word;

He'll defend you,
Fear ye not to follow him.

3 Hear the Savior saying to you,
From his glorious throne above,
"Ye who trust in me for pardon,
By obedience show your love.
Be baptized,
My example points the way."

4 Lord, our hearts incline to follow,
In the way which thou didst tread;
We will turn from every other,
While thy sacred word we read;
O Redeemer,
We rejoice to follow thee.

78 L. M.

BEHOLD the grave where Jesus lay,
Before he shed his precious blood!
How plain he mark'd the humble way
To sinners through the mystic flood!

2 Come, ye redeemed of the Lord,
Come, and obey his sacred word;
He died and rose again for you;
What more could the Redeemer do?

3 Eternal Spirit, heavenly Dove,
On these baptismal waters move;
That we, through energy divine,
May have the substance with the sign.

4 All ye that love Immanuel's name,
And long to feel th' increasing flame,
'Tis you, ye children of the light,
The spirit and the bride invite.

79 C. M.

THERE'S not a bright and beaming smile,
Which in this world I see,
But turns my heart to future joy,
And whispers "heaven" to me.
Though often here my soul is sad,
And falls the silent tear,
There is a world where all are glad,
And sorrow dwells not there.

2 I never clasp a friendly hand,
In greeting, or farewell,
But thoughts of an eternal home
Within my bosom swell:
A prayer to meet in heaven at last
Where all the ransomed come,
And where eternal ages still
Shall find us all at home.

80 C. M.

IN all my Lord's appointed ways,
My journey I'll pursue;
Hinder me not ye much lov'd saints,
For I must go with you.

2 Through floods and flames, if Jesus lead,
I'll follow where he goes:
Hinder me not shall be my cry,
Though earth and hell oppose.

3 Through duty, and through trials too,
I'll go at his command;
Hinder me not, for I am bound
To my Immanuel's land.

4 And when my Savior calls me home,
Still this my cry shall be,
Hinder me not, come welcome death,
I'll gladly go with thee.

81 C. M.

SINCE man by sin, has lost his God
He seeks creation through,
And vainly hopes for solid bliss,
In trying something new.

2 The new possessed, like fading flowers,
Soon loses its gay hue;
The bubble now no longer takes,
The soul wants something new.

3 And could we call all Europe ours,
With India and Peru;
The mind would feel an aching void,
And still want something new.

4 But when we feel the Savior's power,
All good in him we view,

The soul forsakes its vain pursuit,
  Nor seeks for something new.

5 The joys a dear Redeemer brings,
  Will bear a strict review,
Nor need we ever change again,
  For Christ is always new.

82 P. M.

BURST ye emerald gates and bring
  To my raptur'd vision,
All the extatic joys that spring
  Round the bright elysian:
Lo! we lift our longing eyes,
Break, ye intervening skies:
Sun of righteousness, arise,
Ope the gates of paradise.

CHORUS.

O how good it is to be blest,
And dwell where loving Jesus is.

2 Floods of everlasting light
  Freely flash before him,
Myriads with supreme delight,
  Instantly adore him.
Angels' trumps resound his fame;
Lutes of lucid gold proclaim
All the music of his name;
Heaven echoing the theme.

3 Four and twenty elders rise
  From their princely station;

Shout his glorious victories,
Sing the great salvation;
Cast their crowns before his throne;
Cry in reverential tone,
Glory be to God alone!
Holy! Holy! Holy One.

4 One broad rainbow round the throne,
Pours celestial splendor,
All within the brilliant zone,
Is imperial grandeur;
Heaven's pure arch reflects the blaze,
Seraphs sing, admire and gaze;
Glowing cherubs join the lays,
Martyrs shout responding praise.

5 Hark, the thrilling symphonies
Seem, methinks, to seize us;
Join we too the holy lays,
Jesus! Jesus! Jesus!
Sweetest sound in seraph's song,
Sweetest note on mortal's tongue,
Sweetest carol ever sung,
Jesus! Jesus! flow along.

83

L. M.

WHAT various hind'rances we meet,
In coming to the mercy seat;
Yet who that knows the worth of prayer,
But wishes to be often there.

2 Prayer makes the darkest cloud withdraw,
Prayer climbs the ladder Jacob saw;

Gives exercise to faith and love,
Brings every blessing from above.

3 Restraining prayer, we cease to fight,
Prayer makes the Christian's armor bright,
And Satan trembles when he sees
The weakest saint upon his knees.

4 While Moses stood with arms spread wide,
Success was found on Israel's side;
But when through weariness they fail'd,
That moment Amalek prevail'd.

5 Have you no words? Ah think again,
Words flow apace when you complain,
And fill your fellow creature's ear
With the sad tale of all your care.

6 Were half the breath thus vainly spent,
To heaven in supplication sent,
Your cheerful song would oft'ner be,
" Hear what the Lord has done for me."

84

P. M.

THE pearl that worldlings covet,
Is not the pearl for me;
Its beauties fade as quickly,
As sunshine on the sea;
But there's a pearl whose beauty
Fades not, tho' bright it be;
But few its value see,
Oh! that's the pearl for me.

2 The crown that decks the monarch,
Is not the crown for me;
It dazzles but a moment,
Its brightness soon will flee;
But there's a crown whose radiance
No mortal eye can see;
For ever, ever shining—
Oh! that's the crown for me.

3 The road that many travel,
Is not the road for me;
It leads to death and sorrow,
In it I would not be.
But there's a road, tho' narrow,
Hath pleasures rich and free;
'Tis marked by Jesus' footsteps,
Oh! that's the road for me.

4 The hope that sinners cherish,
Is not the hope for me;
Most surely will they perish,
Unless from sin made free;
But there's a hope that calmeth
The waves of life's dark sea,
It pointeth up to heaven—
Oh! that's the hope for me.

85

7s. & 6s.

HOW lost was my condition
Till Jesus made me whole!
There is but one Physician
Can cure the sin-sick soul!

Next door to death he found me,
  And snatched me from the grave,
To tell to all around me,
  His wondrous power to save.

2 The worst of all diseases,
  Is light compared with sin;
On every part it seizes,
  But rages most within.
'T is palsy, plague and fever
  And madness, all combin'd;
And none but a believer,
  The least relief can find.

3 From men great skill professing,
  I thought a cure to gain;
But this proved more distressing,
  And added to my pain:
Some said that nothing ailed me,
  Some gave me up for lost;
Thus every refuge fail'd me,
  And all my hopes were cross'd.

4 At length this great Physician,
  (How matchless is his grace!)
Accepted my petition,
  And undertook my case:
He gave me sight to view him,
  For sin my eyes had sealed;
Then bade me look unto him,
  I looked—and I was heal'd.

5 A risen living Jesus,
  Seen by an eye of faith,

At once from danger frees us,
And saves the soul from death;
Come then to this Physician,
His help he'll freely give;
He makes no hard condition,
'T is only look and live.

86 L. M.

SAY, sinner, hath a voice within,
Oft whispered to thy secret soul,
Urg'd thee to leave the ways of sin,
And yield thy heart to God's control?

2 Hath something met thee in the path
Of worldliness and vanity,
And pointed to the coming wrath,
And warned thee from that wrath to flee?

3 Spurn not the call to life and light;
Regard in time the warning kind;
That call thou mayest not always slight,
And yet the gate of mercy find.

4 Sinner—perhaps this very day,
Thy last accepted time may be;
Oh, shouldst thou grieve him now away,
Then hope may never beam on thee.

87 L. M.

LIFT up your hearts, Immanuel's friends,
And taste the pleasures Jesus sends;
Let nothing cause you to delay,
But hasten on the good old way.

2 Our conflicts here, tho' great they be,
Shall not prevent our victory,
If we but watch and strive and pray,
Like soldiers in the good old way.

3 O, good old way, how sweet thou art!
May none of us from thee depart;
But may our actions always say,
We're marching in the good old way.

4 And when on Pisgah's top we stand,
And view by faith the promis'd land,
Then we may sing, and shout and pray,
And march along the good old way.

5 Ye valiant souls, for heaven contend,
Remember glory's at the end;
Our God will wipe all tears away,
When we have run the good old way.

6 Then far beyond this mortal shore,
We'll meet with those who've gone before,
And shout to think we've gain'd the day,
By marching in the good old way.

88 C. M.

O FOR a heart that loves to pray,
To converse with the Lord,
Fain would I give myself away,
And lean upon his word.

2 O for invigorating grace,
To raise my soul above

O for that heavenly-mindedness
That satan cannot move.

3 O for that fortitude which can
My every fear control;
Then would the dread of sinful men
No more disturb my soul.

4 Lord, thou canst conquer every foe,—
Thy grace can sanctify;
Amen! O Lord, may it be so,
Let my corruptions die.

89 C. M.

BEFORE thy throne, O Lord, we bow
And humbly look to thee:
Let worldly care be banished now,
Let all that's earthly flee.

2 Our feeble wandering minds incite,
To ask the things we ought;
And teach us, Lord, to ask aright.
Else all our prayers are nought.

3 As the disciples asked of old,
O Lord, our faith increase;
O fill our hearts, so dull and cold,
With heavenly love and peace.

4 Make us our nothingness to feel—
Frail creatures of the dust—
Make us submissive to thy will;
Lead us in Thee to trust.

5 While through a glass we darkly see
Thy glories here below,
Prepare us, Lord, to dwell with thee,
And all thy fullness know.

90 L. M.

JESUS! and shall it ever be
A mortal man ashamed of thee!
Ashamed of thee whom angels praise,
Whose glories shine through endless days!

2 Asham'd of Jesus! sooner far
Let evening blush to own a star;
He sheds the beams of light divine,
O'er this benighted soul of mine.

3 Asham'd of Jesus! just as soon
Let midnight be ashamed of noon!
'Tis midnight with my soul till he,
Bright morning star, bids darkness flee.

4 Asham'd of Jesus! that dear friend,
On whom my hopes of heaven depend!
No! when I blush be this my shame,
That I no more revere his name.

5 Asham'd of Jesus! yes I may,
When I've no guilt to wash away;
No tears to wipe, no good to crave,
No fears to quell, no soul to save.

6 Till then, nor is my boasting vain,
Till then, I boast a Savior slain;

And O may this my glory be,
That Christ is not asham'd of me.

91

C. M.

SINNERS, this solemn truth regard,
Hear all ye sons of men;
For Christ the Savior hath declared,
"Ye must be born again."

2 What'er might be your birth or blood,
The sinner's boast is vain;
Thus saith the glorious Son of God,
"Ye must be born again."

3 Our nature's totally depraved,—
The heart a sink of sin;
Without a change, we can't be saved;
"Ye must be born again."

4 Spirit of Life, thy grace impart,
And breathe on sinners slain;
Bear witness, Lord, in every heart,
That we are born again.

92

C M.

LIFT up your hearts to things above,
Ye followers of the Lamb;
And join with us to praise his love,
And glorify his name.

2 To Jesus' name give thanks and sing,
Whose mercies never end:
Rejoice! rejoice! the Lord is King,
The King is now our friend.

3 We for his sake count all things loss,
On earthly good look down,
And joyfully sustain the cross,
Till we receive the crown.

4 O let us stir each other up,
Our faith by works t' approve;
By holy purifying hope,
And the sweet task of love.

5 Let all who for the promise wait,
The Holy Ghost receive;
And rais'd to our unsinning state,
With God in Eden live.

6 Live till the Lord in glory come,
And wait his heav'n to share;
He now is fitting up your home,—
Go on, we'll meet you there.

93

8s. & 7s.

HAIL, ye sighing sons of sorrow,
View with me th' Autumnal gloom,
Learn from thence your fate to-morrow,
Dead, perhaps laid in the tomb.
See all nature fading, dying,
Silent all things seem to mourn,
Life from vegetation flying,
Brings to mind the mould'ring urn.

2 What to me are autumn's treasures,
Since I know no earthly joy,
Long I've lost all earthly pleasures,
Time must youth and health destroy.

Pleasures once I fondly courted,
Shared each bliss that youth bestows,
But to see where then I sported,
Now embitters all my woes.

3 Age and sorrow since have blasted,
Every youthful, pleasing dream;
Quiv'ring age, with youth contrasted,
Oh, how short their glories seem!
As the annual frosts are cropping
Leaves and tendrils from the trees,
So my friends are yearly dropping
Through old age and dire disease.

4 Former friends, how oft I've sought them,
Just to cheer my drooping mind,
But they've gone like leaves in autumn,
Driven before the dreary wind.
When a few more years I've wasted,
When a few more springs are o'er,
When a few more griefs I've tasted,
I shall live to die no more.

5 Fast my sun of life's declining,
I must sleep in death's dark night;
But my hope, pure and refining,
Rests in future life and light.
Cease this trembling, fearing, sighing,
Christ will burst the silent tomb,
Then the saints shall, upwards flying,
Rise into immortal bloom.

94 C. M.

AND let this feeble body fail,
  And let it faint and die;
My soul shall quit this mournful vale,
  And soar to worlds on high:
Shall join the disembodied saints,
  And find its long sought rest;
That only bliss for which it pants,
  In the Redeemer's breast.

2 In hope of that immortal crown,
  I now the cross sustain:
And gladly wander up and down,
  And smile at toil and pain.
I suffer on my threescore years,
  Till my deliverer come;
And wipe away his servant's tears,
  And take his exile home.

3 O what hath Jesus bought for me
  Before my ravished eyes?
Rivers of life divine I see,
  And trees of paradise.
I see a world of spirits bright,
  Who taste the pleasures there;
They all are robed in spotless white,
  And conquering palms they bear.

4 O what are all my suff'rings here,
  If Lord thou count me meet,
With that enraptured host t' appear,
  And worship at thy feet!

Give joy or grief, give ease or pain,
 Take life or friends away ;
But let me meet them all again,
 In that eternal day.

95

7s. & 5s.

HARK! what cry arrests my ear,
 Hark! what accents of despair,
'Tis the heathen's dying prayer;
  Friends of Jesus, hear.

2 Men of God to you we cry,
Rests on you our tearful eye,
Help us, Christians, or we die,
  Die in dark despair.

3 Hasten, Christians, haste to save,
O'er the land and o'er the wave,
Dangers, death, and distance brave,
  Hark ! for help they call.

4 Afric bends her suppliant knee,
Asia spreads her hands to thee,
Hark ! they urge the heaven-born plea,
  Jesus died for all.

5 Haste then, spread the Savior's name,
Snatch the firebrands from the flame,
Deck his glorious diadem
  With their ransom'd souls.

6 See ! the pagan altars fall,
See ! the Savior reigns o'er all ;
Crown him ! crown him ! Lord of all,
  Echoes round the pole.

96

8s. & 7s.

FLY, thou heavenly gospel message,
Fly to yonder foreign lands;
Let the Savior's promis'd blessing,
Reach the distant heathen bands.

2 Go, ye heralds of salvation,
Tell the heathen far and wide,
Jesus bled to save lost sinners
Of each nation, tongue and tribe.

3 Then shall they of heathen nations,
Songs to our Immanuel raise,
In the peaceful realms of glory
Tune their harps to sing his praise.

97

L. M.

GO preach my gospel, saith the Lord;
"Bid the whole earth my grace receive:
He shall be saved that trusts my word,
He shall be damn'd that wont believe.

2 "I'll make your great commission known;
And ye shall prove my gospel true,
By all the works that I have done,
By all the wonders ye shall do.

3 "Teach all the nations my commands;
I'm with you till the world shall end;
All power is trusted in my hands;
I can destroy, and I defend."

4 He spake, and light shone round his head;
On a bright cloud to heaven he rode,
They to the farthest nations spread
The grace of their ascended God.

98

7s. & 6s.

FROM Greenland's icy mountains,
To India's coral strand,
Where Afric's sunny fountains
Roll down their golden sands!
From many an ancient river,
From many a palmy plain,
They call us to deliver
Their land from error's chain.

2 What though the spicy breezes
Blow soft o'er Ceylon's isle;
Though every prospect pleases,
And only man is vile;
In vain with lavish kindness
The gifts of God are strown;
The heathen in his blindness
Bows down to wood and stone.

3 Shall we whose souls are lighted
By wisdom from on high,
Shall we, to men benighted
The lamp of life deny?
Salvation! O Salvation!
The joyful sound proclaim,
Till earth's remotest nation
Has learn'd Messiah's name.

4 Waft, waft, ye winds his story;
And you, ye waters, roll,
Till like a sea of glory,
It spreads from pole to pole;
Till o'er our ransom'd nature,
The Lamb for sinners slain,
Redeemer, King, Creator,
In bliss returns to reign.

99

8s. 7s. & 4s.

YES, my native land, I love thee,
All thy scenes, I love them well;
Friends, connections, happy country,
Must I bid you all farewell!
Can I leave you—
Far in heathen lands to dwell!

2 Home! thy joys are passing lovely!
Joys no stranger heart can tell!
Happy home, indeed I love thee!
Can I—can I say—"Farewell?
Can I leave thee—
Far in heathen lands to dwell!

3 Scenes of sacred peace and pleasure,
Holy days and Sabbath-bell,
Richest, brightest, sweetest treasure!
Can I say a last farewell?
Can I leave you—
Far in heathen lands to dwell?

4 Yes! I hasten from you gladly,
From the scenes I love so well?

Far away, ye billows bear me!
Lovely native land, farewell!
Pleased I leave thee—
Far in heathen lands to dwell.

5 In the deserts let me labor,
On the mountains let me tell
How he died—the blessed Savior—
To redeem a world from hell.
Let me hasten—
Far in heathen lands to dwell.

6 Bear me on thou restless ocean;
Let the winds my canvass swell;
Heaves my heart with warm emotion,
While I go far hence to dwell.
Glad I bid thee,
Native land! Farewell, Farewell.

100 H. M.

BLOW ye the trumpet, blow,
The gladly solemn sound,
Let all the nations know,
To earth's remotest bound:
The year of Jubilee is come;
Return, ye ransom'd sinners, home.

2 Exalt the Lamb of God,
The sin atoning Lamb;
Redemption by his blood,
Through all the lands proclaim:
The year of Jubilee is come;
Return, ye ransom'd sinners, home.

3 Ye slaves of sin and hell,
Your liberty receive:
And safe in Jesus dwell,
And blest in Jesus live:
The year of Jubilee is come;
Return, ye ransom'd sinners, home.

4 The gospel trumpet hear,
The news of pardoning grace;
Ye favored souls draw near;
Behold your Savior's face:
The year of Jubilee has come;
Return, ye ransom'd sinners, home.

5 Jesus, our great High Priest,
Hath full atonement made;
Ye weary spirits rest,
Ye mournful souls be glad:
The year of Jubilee has come;
Return, ye ransom'd sinners, home.

101

7s.

WATCHMAN! tell us of the night,
What its signs of promise are.
Traveller! o'er yon mountain's height,
See that glory beaming star!
Watchman! does its beauteous ray
Aught of hope or joy foretell?
Traveller! yes, it brings the day,
Promised day of Israel.

2 Watchman, tell us of the night,
Higher yet that star ascends

Traveller! blessedness and light,
  Peace and truth, its course portends!
Watchman! will its beams alone
  Gild the spot that gave them birth?
Traveller! ages are its own,
  See, it bursts o'er all the earth.

3 Watchman! tell us of the night,
  For the morning seems to dawn.
Traveller! darkness takes its flight;
  Doubt and terror are withdrawn.
Watchman! let thy wanderings cease,
  Hie thee to thy quiet home.
Traveller! lo! the prince of peace,
  Lo the Son of God is come.

102 C. M.

HAIL sweetest, dearest tie that binds
  Our glowing hearts in one,
Hail! sacred hope that tunes our minds
  To harmony divine.

CHORUS.

It is the hope, the blissful hope,
  Which Jesus' grace hath given;
The hope when days and years are past,
  We all shall meet in heaven;
We all shall meet in heaven at last,
  We all shall meet in heaven;
The hope when days and years are past,
  We all shall meet in heaven.

2 What though the northern wintry blast,
  Shall howl around thy cot:

What! though beneath an eastern sky
Be cast our distant lot.
Yet still we share the blissful hope, &c.

3 From Burmah's shores, from Afric's strand,
From India's burning plain,
From Europe, from Columbia's land,
We hope to meet again.
It is the hope, the blissful hope, &c.

4 No lingering look, no parting sigh,
Our future meeting knows:
There friendship beams from every eye,
And hope immortal glows.
O sacred hope! O blissful hope, &c.

103 *Burial of Mrs. Judson.*

MOURNFULLY, tenderly,
Bear on the dead,
Where the warrior has lain,
Let the Christian be laid;
No place more befitting—
O Rock of the sea!
Never such treasure
Was hidden in thee.

2 Mournfully, tenderly,
Solemn and slow,
Tears are bedewing
The path as ye go;
Kindred and strangers,
Are mourners to-day,
Gently, so gently,
O! bear her away.

3 Mournfully, tenderly,
Gaze on that brow,
Beautiful is it
In quietude now:
One look! and then settle
The loved to her rest,
The ocean beneath her,
The turf on her breast.

4 So have ye buried her—
Up! and depart,
To life and to duty
With undismayed heart:
Fear not—for the love
Of the stranger will keep,
The casket that lies
In the Rock of the deep.

5 Peace! to thy bosom,
Thou servant of God!
The vale thou art treading,
Before, thou hast trod:
Precious dust thou hast laid
By the Hopia tree,
And treasure as precious
In the Rock of the sea!

104

7s. & 6s.

THE morning light is breaking,
The darkness disappears;
The sons of earth are waking
To penitential tears:

Each breeze that sweeps the ocean
  Brings tiding from afar
Of nations in commotion,
  Prepared for Zion's war.

2 Rich dews of grace come o'er us,
  In many a gentle shower,
And brighter scenes before us
  Are opening every hour;
Each cry to heaven going,
  Abundant answers brings,
And heavenly gales are blowing,
  With peace upon their wings.

3 See heathen nations bending
  Before the God we love,
And thousand hearts ascending
  In gratitude above;
While sinners, now confessing,
  The gospel call obey,
And seek the Savior's blessing,—
  A nation in a day.

105 H. M.

RISE, Sun of glory, rise,
  And chase the shades of night,
Which now obscure the skies,
  And hide thy sacred light:
O, chase those dismal shades away,
And bring the bright, millennial day!

2 Now send thy spirit down
  On all the nations, Lord,

With great success to crown
The preaching of thy word;
That heathen lands may own thy sway,
And cast their idol gods away.

3 Then shall thy kingdom come
Among our fallen race,
And all the earth become
The temple of thy grace;
Whence pure devotion shall ascend,
And songs of praise till time shall end.

106

8s. 7s. & 4s.

WHO but thou, almighty Spirit,
Can the heathen world reclaim?
Men can preach, but till thou favor,
Heathens will be still the same,
Mighty Spirit!
Witness to the Savior's name.

2 Thou hast promised by the prophets,
Glorious light in latter days;
Come and bless bewildered nations,
Change our prayers and tears to praise;
Promised Spirit!
Round the world diffuse thy rays.

3 All our hopes, and prayers, and labors
Must be vain without thine aid;
But thou wilt not disappoint us,
All is true that thou hast said;
Faithful Spirit!
O'er the world thine influence shed.

107

C. M.

HOW happy is the man who hears
  Religion's warning voice,
And who celestial wisdom makes
  His early, only choice.

2 Religion is the chief concern,
  Of mortals here below;
May I its great importance learn,
  Its sovereign virtue know!

3 More needful this than glittering wealth,
  Or aught the world bestows;
Nor reputation, food, or health,
  Can give us such repose.

4 Religion should our thoughts engage,
  Amidst our youthful bloom:
'T will fit us for declining age,
  And for the awful tomb.

108

7s. & 5s. Double.

FRIENDS, for whom a Savior died,
  Friends, who have a heavenly Guide,
Welcome here, for side by side,
  We must take our stand:
Now 's the hour for us to meet,
Girt in panoply complete,
Sharing in communion sweet,
  An immortal band.

2 See ye not the world is set,
Hostile to salvation yet;

Heed ye not the subtle net,
By the tempter spread:
Know ye not the senses still
War against the hallow'd will,
Aiming all the heart to fill?
Will ye be misled?

3 Friends, to holy conflict wake;
Every spell of ruin break:
Rouse ye for the Savior's sake,
Can ye slumber more?
Arm! the standard blazes high—
Hark! 'tis Jesus' battle cry—
On! salvation now is nigh—
Rest forevermore!

109

9s. 8s. & 11s.

SEE, brothers, see! how the day rolls on,
Soon we'll hail the rising sun,
Hark! 'tis the spirit's warning voice,
Lift your heads, ye saints rejoice!

2 See, brothers, see! how the day comes on,
Soon the trump of God will sound!
Lightnings may flash, and thunders roll,
Welcome to the faithful soul!

3 Hark! 'tis the trumpet's joyful sound!
See the Almighty Jesus crowned!
Saints of the Lord, awake, arise!
Bid him welcome from the skies.

CHORUS.

Then haste, let us work till probation is o'er,
We go to the land where our toiling is o'er,

Our earthly labor being done,
How sweet the Christian's welcome home.

Home, home, home! the Christian's welcome home!
Sweet, oh sweet the Christian's welcome home.
Welcome home, welcome home, welcome home.

110 C. M.

THERE is a fountain filled with blood,
Drawn from Immanuel's veins;
And sinners plunged beneath that flood,
Lose all their guilty stains.

2 The dying thief rejoic'd to see
That fountain in his day;
And there may I, though vile as he,
Wash all my sins away.

3 Dear dying Lamb, thy precious blood
Shall never lose its power,
Till all the ransom'd church of God
Are saved, to sin no more.

4 E'er since, by faith I saw the stream,
Thy flowing wounds supply,
Redeeming love has been my theme,
And shall be, till I die.

5 And when this feeble, stammering tongue
Lies silent in the grave,

Then, in a nobler, sweeter song,
I'll sing thy power to save.

111 7s. & 4s.

I'M a lonely trav'ler here,
Weary, opprest;
But my journey's end is near—
Soon I shall rest.
Dark and dreary is the way,
Toiling I've come—
Ask me not with you to stay,
Yonder 's my home.

2 I'm a weary trav'ler here,
I must go on,
For my journey's end is near—
I must be gone.
Brighter joys than earth can give,
Win me away;
Pleasures that forever live,—
I cannot stay.

3 I'm a trav'ler to a land
Where all is fair;
Where is seen no broken band,
Saints, all are there.
Where no tears shall ever fall,
Nor heart be sad;
Where the glory is for all,
And all are glad.

4 I'm a trav'ler, and I go,
Where all is fair;

Farewell all I've loved below—
  I must be there.
Worldly honors, hopes and gain,
  All I resign;
Welcome sorrow, grief and pain,
  If heaven be mine!

I'm a trav'ler, call me not—
  Upward 's my way;
Yonder is my rest and lot,
  I cannot stay.
Farewell earthly pleasures all,
  Pilgrim I roam;
Hail me not, in vain you call,
  Yonder 's my home.

12

8s. & 7s.

THIS world is all a fleeting show
  For man's illusion given;
The smiles of joy, the tears of wo,
Deceitful shine, deceitful flow;
  There's nothing true but Heaven.

As false the light on glory's plume,
  As fading hues at even;
And genius' bud and beauty's bloom,
Are blossoms gathered for the tomb,
  There's nothing bright but Heaven.

Poor wanderers on a stormy sea,
  From wave to wave we're driven;
And fancy's flash, and reason's ray

Serve but to light us on the way;
 There's nothing calm but Heaven.

4 And where's the hand held out to cheer
 The heart with anguish riven?
For sorrow's sigh, and trouble's tear
Have never found a refuge here;
 There's nothing kind but Heaven.

5 In vain do mortals sigh for bliss,
 Without their sins forgiven;
True pleasure, everlasting peace,
Are only found in God's free grace;
 There's nothing good but heaven.

6 From such as walk in wisdom's road,
 Corroding fears are driven;
They're washed in Christ's atoning blood
Enjoy communion with their God,
 And find their way to heaven.

113 C. M.

HARK! listen to the trumpeters,
 They call for volunteers,
On Zion's bright and holy mount,
 Behold the officers.

2 Their horses white, their armor bright,
 With courage bold they stand,
Enlisting soldiers for the fight,
 To march to Canaan's land.

3 They follow their great General,
 The great eternal Lamb,

is garments stain'd in his own blood,
King Jesus is his name.

'he trumpets sound, the armies shout,
They drive the hosts of hell:
low dreadful is our God t' adore,
The great Immanuel!

inners, enlist with Jesus Christ,
The eternal Son of God;
nd march with us to Canaan's land,
Beyond the swelling flood.

ift up your heads, ye soldiers bold,
Redemption's drawing nigh;
Ve soon shall hear the trumpet sound,
That shakes the earth and sky.

n fiery chariots we shall rise,
And leave the world on fire:
And all surround the throne of love,
And join the heavenly choir.

14 C. P. M.

WHAT sound is this salutes my ear?
'Tis Gabriel's trump methinks I hear,
'Tis Gabriel's trump methinks I hear,
The expected day is come.
Behold the heavens, the earth, the sea,
Proclaim the year of Jubilee,
Proclaim the year of Jubilee;
Return ye exiles home.

2 Behold the fair Jerusalem,
Illuminated by the Lamb,
In glory doth appear.
Fair Zion rising from the tombs,
To meet the Bridegroom—lo! he comes,
And hails the festive year.

3 My soul is striving to be there,
I long to rise and wing the air,
And trace the sacred road.
Adieu, adieu, all earthly things;
O that I had an angel's wings,
I'd quickly see my God.

4 Fly, lingering moments, fly, O fly,
I thirst, I pant, I long to try
Angelic joys to prove!
Soon shall I quit this house of clay,
Clap my glad wings and soar away,
And shout redeeming love.

115 C M.

ARISE and shine, O Zion fair,
Behold thy light is come,
Thy glorious conqu'ring King is near,
To take his exiles home:
The trumpet's thund'ring through the sky
To set poor sinners free;
The day of wonders now is nigh,
The year of Jubilee.

2 Arise ye nations under ground,
Before the Judge appear;

All tongues, all languages, shall come,
  Their final doom to hear.
King Jesus on his azure throne,
  Ten thousand angels round,
While Gabriel with his silver trump,
  Echoes the dreadful sound.

3 The glorious news of gospel grace
  With sinners now is o'er;
The trump of Zion now is still,
  And to be blown no more;
The watchmen have all left their walls,
  And with their flocks above
On Canaan's happy shore they sing,
  And shout redeeming love.

4 Come all ye pilgrims of the Lord,
  Whose hearts are joined in one:
Hold up your heads with courage bold,
  Your race is almost run;
Above the clouds behold him stand,
  And smiling, bid you come;
Whilst angels beckon you away,
  To your eternal home.

5 To see a pilgrim as he dies,
  With glory in his view!
To heaven he lifts his longing eyes,
  And bids the world adieu!
While friends stand weeping all around,
  And loth to let him go,
He shouts with his expiring breath,
  And leaves them all below.

6 O Christians! are you ready now,
To cross the narrow flood?
On Canaan's happy shore behold,
And see a smiling God!
The dazzling charms of that bright world,
Attract my soul above;
My tongue shall shout redeeming grace,
When perfected in love.

116

8s. & 7s.

MERCY, O thou son of David,
Thus blind Bartimeus pray'd;
Many by thy grace are saved,
O wilt thou vouchsafe thine aid!

2 Lord, remove this grievous blindness,
Turn my darkness into day;
Straight he saw, and drawn by kindness,
Follow'd Jesus in the way.

3 Now methinks I hear him praising,
Publishing to all around,
Friends, is not my case amazing?
What a Savior I have found.

4 O that all the blind but knew him,
And would be advised by me;
Surely they would come unto him,
He would cause them all to see.

117

7s. & 6s.

CALL'D to a sense of duty,
I would obey the call;

And for the sake of Jesus.
I freely give up all
My former vain enjoyments,
Of pleasure, pride and gain;
That I in Jesus' kingdom
A mansion may obtain.

2 Come, who will travel with me,
The way that leads to heaven,
And follow none but Jesus,
The way which he hath given:
And take his word for counsel,
His spirit for a guide;
And make a full surrender
Of every thing beside?

3 Come on, my precious brethren,
And travel on with me;
We'll seek for heav'nly treasure,
Until we find the sea
Of sweet unbounded riches,
Of life, and love, and peace:
Where beauty never withers,
And glories never cease.

4 What though the world reproach us,
And say we're mean and poor;
No matter what we suffer,
If we can reach the shore:
'T will make the glory sweeter,
And raise the praises higher;
And we shall be completer.
When purified by fire.

8

118 C. M.

ALL hail the power of Jesus' name,
Let angels prostrate fall:
Bring forth the royal diadem,
And crown him Lord of all.

2 Ye chosen seed of Israel's race,
A remnant weak and small:
Hail him who saves you by his grace,
And crown him Lord of all.

3 Ye Gentile sinners, ne'er forget
The wormwood and the gall;
Go—spread your trophies at his feet,
And crown him Lord of all.

4 O, that with yonder sacred throng,
We at his feet may fall;
We'll join the everlasting song,
And crown him Lord of all.

119 P. M.

STOP, poor sinner, stop and think
Before you farther go,
Can you sport upon the brink
Of everlasting woe?
Hell beneath is gaping wide,
Vengeance waits the dread command,
Soon to stop your sport and pride,
And sink you with the damn'd

CHORUS.

Then be entreated now to stop,
For unless you warning take,
Ere you are aware you'll drop
Into a burning lake.

2 Say, have you an arm like God,
That you his will oppose?
Fear you not that iron rod
With which he breaks his foes?
Can you stand in that great day,
When his judgment will proclaim—
And the earth shall melt away,
Like wax before the flame?

3 Ghastly death will quickly come,
And drag you to the bar;
Then to hear your awful doom,
Will fill you with despair.
All your sins will round you crowd,
Sins of a blood-crimson dye;
Each for vengeance cry aloud,
And what will you reply?

4 Though your hearts be made of steel,
Your forehead lined with brass,
God at length will make you feel,
He will not let you pass.
Sinners then in vain will call,
Though they now despise his grace,
Rocks and mountains on us fall,
And hide us from his face.

5 But as yet there is a hope,
You may his mercy know;

Though his arm be lifted up,
He still forbears the blow.
'T was for sinners Jesus died;
Sinners he invites to come;
None that come shall be denied,
He says, there still is room.
For Jesus' sake, I pray you stop, &c.

120 C. M.

I'M on my way to Canaan,
I'll bid the world farewell;
Come on my fellow travellers,
In spite of earth and hell.
Though Satan's army rages,
And all his hosts combine;
Yet Scripture doth engage us,
The strength of love divine.

2 I'll blow the gospel trumpet—
On all the nations call;
For Christ hath me commissioned,
To say he died for all.
Come, try his grace and prove him,
You shall a gift obtain—
He will not send you empty,
Nor let you come in vain.

3 But if you want a witness,
We have one just at hand,
Who lately has experienced,
The glories of the land.

It comes in copious showers,
  Our bodies can't contain;
It fills our ransom'd powers,
  And still we drink again.

121 7s. & 6s.

GO when the morning shineth,
  Go when the noon is bright;
Go when the eve declineth,
  Go in the hush of night,
Go with pure mind and feeling,
  Fling earthly thought away,
And in thy chamber kneeling,
  Do thou in secret pray.

2 Remember all who love thee—
  All who are loved by thee:
Pray, too, for those who hate thee,
  If any such there be;
Then for thyself in meekness
  A blessing humbly claim,
And link with each petition
  Thy great Redeemer's name.

3 Or if 'tis e'er denied thee
  In solitude to pray,
Should holy tho'ts come o'er thee
  When friends are round thy way,
E'en then the silent breathing
  Of thy spirit raised above,
Will reach his throne of glory,
  Who is mercy, truth, and love.

4 Oh not a joy or blessing
With this can we compare—
The power that he hath given us,
To pour our souls in prayer;
Whene'er thou pinest in sadness,
Before his footstool fall,
And remember in thy gladness
His grace who gave thee all.

122

7s.

SINNERS, turn, why will you die?
God, your Maker, asks you why?
God, who did your being give,
Made you with himself to live;
He the fatal cause demands,
Asks the work of his own hands;
Why, ye thankless creatures, why
Will ye cross his love, and die?

2 Sinners, turn, why will ye die?
Christ your Savior, asks you why;
He who did your souls retrieve,
Died himself that ye might live,
Will you let him die in vain?
Crucify your Lord again?
Why, ye ransomed sinners, why
Will you slight his grace, and die?

3 Sinners, turn, why will you die?
God, the Spirit, asks you why?
He who all your lives hath strove,
Wooed you to embrace his love.

Will ye not his grace receive ?
Will ye still refuse to live ?
Why, ye long sought sinners, why
Will you grieve your God, and die ?

123 P. M.

HOW sweet to reflect on those joys that await me
In yon blissful region, the haven of rest;
Where glorified spirits with welcome shall greet me
And lead me to mansions prepared for the blest;
Encircled in light, and with glory enshrouded,
My happiness perfect, my mind's sky unclouded,
I'll bathe in the ocean of pleasure unbounded,
And range with delight through the Eden of Love.

2 While angelic legions, with harps tuned celestial,
Harmoniously join in the concert of praise,
The saints, as they flock from the regions terrestrial,
In loud hallelujahs their voices shall raise:
Then songs to the Lamb shall re-echo thro' heav'n,
My soul will respond, to Immanuel be given
All glory, all honor, all might and dominion,
Who brought us through grace to the Eden of Love.

3 Then hail, blessed state! Hail ye songsters of glory!
Ye harpers of bliss, soon I'll meet you above!
And join your full choir in rehearsing the story,
Salvation from sorrow, through Jesus' love,
Though 'prisoned in earth, yet by anticipation,
Already my soul feels a sweet prelibation,
Of joys that await me, when freed from probation,
My heart's now in heaven, the Eden of Love.

124 8s. 7s. & 4s.

SEE the eternal Judge descending—
View him seated on his throne!

Now, poor sinner, now, lamenting,
Stand and hear thy awful doom
Trumpets call thee;
Stand and hear thy awful doom.

2 Hear the cries he now is venting,
Filled with dread of fiercer pain;
While in anguish thus lamenting,
That he ne'er was born again—
Greatly mourning,
That he ne'er was born again

3 Yonder sits my slighted Savior,
With the marks of dying love;
O, that I had sought his favor,
When I felt his spirit move—
Golden moments,
When I felt his spirit move!

4 Now despisers, look and wonder;
Hope and sinners here must part;
Louder than a peal of thunder,
Hear the dreadful sound, "Depart!"
Lost forever,—
Hear the dreadful sound, "Depart."

125 L. M.

AWAKE, my soul, to joyful lays,
And sing the great Redeemer's praise;
He justly claims a song from me:
His loving kindness, O how free!

2 Ye saw me ruined by the fall,
Yet loved me, notwithstanding all;

He saved me from my lost estate.
His loving kindness, O how great!

3 Though numerous hosts of mighty foes,
Though earth and hell, my way oppose,
He safely leads my soul along:
His loving kindness, O how strong?

4 When trouble like a gloomy cloud,
Has gathered thick and thunder'd loud,
He near my soul has always stood:
His loving kindness, O how good!

5 I often feel my sinful heart
Prone from my Jesus to depart;
But though I oft have him forgot,
His loving kindness changes not.

6 Soon shall I pass the gloomy vale;
Soon all my mortal powers must fail;
O, may my last, expiring breath
His loving kindness sing in death.

7 Then let me mount and soar away
To the bright world of endless day,
And sing with rapture and surprise,
His loving kindness in the skies.

126 C. M.

COME, let us use the grace divine,
And all with one accord,
In a perpetual cov'nant, join
Ourselves to Christ the Lord.

2 Give up ourselves through Jesus' power;
His name to glorify;
And promise in this sacred hour,
For God to live and die.

3 The cov'nant we this moment make
Be ever kept in mind;
We will no more our God forsake,
Or cast his words behind.

4 We never will throw off his fear,
Who hears our solemn vow;
And if thou art well pleased to hear,
Come down and meet us now!

127 P. M.

O CARELESS sinner, come,
Pray now attend;
This world is not your home,
It soon will end.
Jehovah calls aloud,
Forsake the thoughtless crowd;
Pursue the road to God,
And happy be.

2 No happiness you'll find,
While thus you go;
No peace unto your mind,
But pain and wo
Attend you every day,
While far from God you stray;
O sinner, come away,
And ever live.

3 How many calls you've had,
I call again,
How can you be so bad,
So full of sin,
As to refuse that voice,
Which calls you to rejoice,
In making heaven your choice,
And shunning hell?

4 Nor do I call alone;
The Savior too,
E'en with his dying groan,
Cries, bid adieu,
To all your lovers now,
And to his sceptre bow,
And he will tell you how
To live anew.

5 But if you will refuse,
Down, down you'll go,
And with the wicked choose
The road to wo;
Alas, how can you slight
The rays of Gospel light,
And sink in endless night,
Where silence reigns?

128 C. M.

LORD, when together here we meet,
And taste thy heavenly grace,
Thy smiles are so divinely sweet,
We're loth to leave the place.

2 But, Father, since it is thy will
That we must part again,

O may thy precious presence still,
With every one remain.

3 And let us all in Christ be one,
Bound with the cords of love;
Till we before thy glorious throne
Shall joyful meet above.

4 All sin and sorrow from each heart
Shall then forever fly;
Nor shall a thought that we must part
Once interrupt our joy.

129

8s. & 7s.

HAIL! thou once despised Jesus,
Hail! thou everlasting king;
Thou didst suffer to redeem us!
Thou didst free salvation bring.
Hail! thou agonizing Savior,
Bearer of our sin and shame!
By thy merits we find favor;
Life is given through thy name.

2 Paschal Lamb, by God appointed,
All our sins on thee were laid;
By almighty love anointed,
Thou hast full atonement made;
All thy people are forgiven,
Through the virtue of thy blood;
Opened is the gate of heaven!
Peace is made 'twixt man and God.

3 Jesus, Hail! enthroned in glory,
There forever to abide!

All the heavenly hosts adore thee,
Seated at thy Father's side ;
There for sinners thou art pleading,
There thou dost our place prepare,
Ever for us interceding,
Till in glory we appear.

Worship, honor, power and blessing,
Thou art worthy to receive;
Loudest praises without ceasing
Meet it is for us to give;
Help, ye bright angelic spirits,
Bring your sweetest, noblest lays;
Help to sing our Savior's merits;
Help to chant Immanuel's praise.

130 S. M.

A CHARGE to keep I have,
A God to glorify;
A never dying soul to save,
And fit it for the sky.

2 To serve the present age;
My calling to fulfil;
O may it all my powers engage,
To do my Master's will.

3 Arm me with jealous care,
As in thy sight to live;
And oh, thy servant, Lord, prepare,
A strict account to give!

4 Help me to watch and pray,
And on thyself rely,

Assured if I my trust betray,
I shall forever die.

131 C. M.

O FOR that tenderness of heart
That bows before the Lord!
That owns how just and good thou art,
And trembles at thy word!

2 O for those humble, contrite tears
Which from repentance flow,
That sense of guilt, which, trembling, fears
The long suspended blow!

3 Savior, to me in pity give
For sin the deep distress;
The pledge thou wilt at last receive,
And bid me die in peace.

4 O, fill my soul with faith and love,
And strength to do thy will;
Raise my desires and hopes above;
Thyself to me reveal.

132 P. M.

WHEN sorrows encompass around,
And deepest distresses I see,
Astonish'd, I cry, can a mortal be found,
That's surrounded with trouble like me!

2 Few moments of peace I enjoy,
And they are succeeded by pain,
If a moment in praising my God I employ,
I have hours again to complain.

3 O when will my sorrows be o'er,
O when will my sufferings cease,
O when to the bosom of Christ shall I soar,
To mansions of glory in peace!

4 O then with the fulness of love,
I there like an angel shall sing
Till Christ shall descend with a shout from above,
And with him his sanctified bring.

5 Our slumbering bodies obey,
And quicker than thought will arise;
Remov'd in a moment go shouting away
To mansions above in the skies.

133

8s. 7s. & 4s.

GUIDE me, O thou great Jehovah,
Pilgrim through this barren land:
I am weak, but thou art mighty;
Hold me with thy powerful hand:
Bread of heaven,
Feed me till I want no more.

2 Open, Lord, the crystal fountain,
Whence the healing waters flow;
Let the fiery, cloudy pillar
Lead me all my journey through:
Strong Deliverer,
Be thou still my strength and shield.

3 When I tread the verge of Jordan,
Bid my anxious fears subside;

Bear me through the swelling current,
Land me safe on Canaan's side:
Songs of praises
I will ever give to thee.

134 C. M.

THERE is a land of pure delight,
Where saints immortal reign;
Infinite day excludes the night,
And pleasures banish pain.

2 There everlasting spring abides,
And never-withering flowers;
Death like a narrow sea divides
This heavenly land from ours.

3 Sweet fields beyond the swelling flood,
Stand dressed in living green;
So to the Jews old Canaan stood,
While Jordan rolled between.

4 But timorous mortals start and shrink
To cross this narrow sea,
And linger, shivering on the brink,
And fear to launch away.

5 O, could we make our doubts remove,
These gloomy doubts that rise,—
And see the Canaan that we love
With unbeclouded eyes.

6 Could we but climb where Moses stood
And view the landscape o'er;

Not Jordan's stream, nor death's cold flood,
Could fright us from the shore.

135 C. M.

HOW can I sleep when angels sing,
And all the saints on high,
Cry glory to the eternal King,
The Lamb that once did die ?

2 For I of all the race that fell,
Or all the heav'nly host,
Have greatest cause with humble soul
To love and praise him most.

3 Did God so love this ruin'd world,
As to bestow his Son
A ransom, sinners to redeem,
And save from wrath to come ?

4 No longer, then, will I repose,
But rise to praise and pray,
And swell the song till night shall close
In an eternal day.

136 C. M.

LET every mortal ear attend,
And every heart rejoice !
The trumpet of the gospel sounds,
With an inviting voice.

2 Ho ! all ye hungry, starving souls,
Who feed upon the wind,

And vainly strive with earthly toys,
To fill an empty mind.

3 Eternal wisdom has prepared
A soul-reviving feast;
And bids your longing appetites
The rich provision taste.

4 Ho! ye who pant for living streams,
And pine away and die;
Here you may quench your raging thirst,
With streams that never dry.

5 The happy gates of gospel grace
Stand open all the day.
Lord, we are come to seek supplies,
A d drive our wants away.

137 C. M.

FAREWELL vain world, I bid adieu,
Your glories I despise;
Your friendship I'll no more pursue,
Your flatt'ries are but lies.

2 You promise happiness in vain,
Nor can you satisfy;
Your highest pleasures turn to pain,
And all your treasures die.

3 Had I the Indies east and west,
And riches of the sea,
Without my God I could not rest,
For he is all to me.

4 Then let my soul rise far above,
By faith I'll take my wing,
To the eternal realms of love,
Where saints and angels sing.

138 7s. 6 Lines.

WHEN shall we all meet again?
When shall we all meet again?
Oft shall glowing hope expire,
Oft shall wearied love retire,
Oft shall death and sorrow reign,
Ere we all shall meet again.

2 Though in distant lands we sigh,
Parch'd beneath a hostile sky;
Though the deep between us rolls,
Friendship shall unite our souls,
And in fancy's wide domain,
Oft shall we all meet again.

3 When our burnish'd locks are gray,
Thin'd by many a toil-spent day;
When around this youthful pine,
Moss shall creep, and ivy twine,
Long may this loved bower remain,
Here may we all meet again.

4 When the dreams of life are fled,
When its wasted lamp is dead,
When in cold oblivion's shade,
Beauty, wealth, and fame are laid—
Where immortal spirits reign,
There may we all meet again.

139 P. M.

THE people called Christians
Have many things they tell,
About the land of Canaan,
Where saints and angels dwell;
But sin, a dreadful ocean,
Encloses them around,
With its tide still divides them,
From Canaan's happy ground.

2 Thousands have been impatient
To find a passage through,
And with united vigor
Have tried what they could do:
But vessels built by human skill
Have never sailed far,
Till we found them aground
On some dreadful sandy bar.

3 The everlasting gospel
Has launch'd to th' deep at last;
Behold her sails extended
Around her towering mast;
Along her deck in order,
Her joyful sailors stand,
Crying, "Ho! here we go
To Immanuel's happy land!

4 To all that stand spectators
What anguish will ensue,
To hear their old companions
Bid them a long adieu;

The pleasure of your paradise
Can us no more invite,
While we sail, you may rail,
But we'll soon be out of sight.

5 We're now on the wide ocean,
We bid this world farewell;
And where we shall cast anchor
No human tongue can tell:
About our future destiny
There needs no more debate,
While we ride on the tide,
With the Captain and his Mate.

6 The passengers united,
In order, peace and love;
The wind all in our favor,
How sweetly we do move;
The tempest now assails us,
The raging billows roar!
We will sweep through the deep,
Till we reach that blessed shore.

140 AIR—*Daughter of Zion.*

CHILDREN of Zion! what harp notes are stealing,
So soft o'er our senses, so soothingly sweet:
'T is the music of angels, their raptures revealing,
That you have been brought to the Holy One's feet.
Children of Zion! We join in their welcome;
'T is sweet to lie low at that blessed retreat.

2 Children of Zion! no longer in sadness,
Refrain from the feast that your Savior hath given;
Come taste of the cup of salvation with gladness,
And think of the banquet still sweeter in heaven.

Children of Zion ! our hearts bid you welcome,
To the church of the ransomed—the kingdom of heaven.

3 Children of Zion ! we joyfully hail you !
Who 've entered the sheepfold through Jesus the door ;
While pilgrims on earth, tho' the foe may assail you,
Press forward, and soon will the conflict be o'er.
Children of Zion ! Oh welcome, thrice welcome !
We'll meet where the foe shall oppress thee no more.

141 L. M.

MY Christian friends in bonds of love,
Whose hearts in sweetest union prove,
Your friendship's like a drawing band,
Yet we must take the parting hand.

2 Your company's sweet, your union's dear,
Your words delightful to my ear ;
And when I see that we must part,
You draw like cords around my heart.

3 How sweet the hours have pass'd away,
When we have met to sing and pray ;
How loth we've been to leave the place
Where Jesus shows his smiling face.

4 O could I stay with friends so kind,
How would it cheer my fainting mind ;
But duty makes me understand
That we must take the parting hand.

5 Then since it is God's holy will
We must be parted for a while,

In sweet submission, all as one,
We'll say, our Father's will be done.

142 L. M.

GO worship at Immanuel's feet,
See, in his Name what wonders meet;
Earth is too narrow to express
His worth, his glory or his grace.

2 The whole creation can afford,
But some faint shadow of my Lord:
Nature, to make his beauties known,
Must mingle colors not her own.

3 Is he a Fountain? There I'll bathe,
And heal the plague of sin and death,
These waters all my soul renew,
And cleanse my spotted garments too.

4 Is he a Sun? His beams are grace,
His course is joy and righteousness—
Is he a tree? The world receives
Salvation from his healing leaves.

5 Is he a Rose? Not Sharon yields
Such fragrancy in all her fields.
Or if the lily he assume
The valleys bless the rich perfume.

6 Is he a Star? He breaks the night
And spreads for all the dawning light—
I know his glories from afar,
I know the bright, the Morning Star.

7 Is he a Way? He leads to God,
The path is drawn in lines of blood!
There would I walk with hope and zeal,
Till I arrive at Zion's hill.

8 Is he a Door? I'll enter in—
Behold the pastures large and green,
A Paradise divinely fair,
And all the saints have freedom there.

9 Is he a Rock? How firm he proves?
The Rock of Ages never moves:
Yet the sweet streams that from him flow,
Attend us all the desert through.

10 Is he designed a Corner-Stone,
For men to build their heaven upon?
I'll make him my foundation too;
Nor fear the plots of hell below.

11 Nor earth, nor seas, nor sun, nor stars,
Nor heaven his full resemblance bears,
His beauties we can never trace,
Till we behold him face to face.

143 L. M.

AWAY my doubts, be gone my fear,
The wonders of the Lord appear;
The wonders which my Savior wrought,
O how delightful is the thought!

2 The wonders of redeeming love,
When first my heart was drawn above,

When first I saw my Savior's face,
And triumph'd in his pard'ning grace.

3 Pursue my thoughts this pleasing theme,
'T was not a fancy nor a dream;
'T was grace descending from the skies,
And shall be marv'lous in my eyes.

4 Long had I mourn'd like one forgot,
Long had my soul for comfort sought,
Jesus was witness to my tears,
And Jesus sweetly calm'd my fears.

5 He cleans'd my soul, he chang'd my dress,
And cloth'd me with his righteousness;
He spake at once my sins forgiven,
And I rejoic'd as if in heaven.

6 These are the wonders I record,
The marv'lous goodness of the Lord,
O for a tongue to speak his praise,
To tell the triumphs of his grace.

144 C. M.

FROM all that's mortal, all that's vain,
And from this earthly clod,
Arise, my soul, and strive to gain
Some fellowship with God.

2 Say, what is there below the sky,
In all the paths thou'st trod,
Can suit thy wishes or thy joys,
Like fellowship with God.

3 Nor life, nor all the toys of art,
Nor pleasure's flowery road,
Can to my soul such bliss impart,
As fellowship with God.

4 When I in love am made to bear
Affliction's needful rod?
Light, sweet and kind it now appears
Thro' fellowship with God.

5 And when the icy arms of death
Shall chill my flowing blood,
With joy I'll yield my latest breath
In fellowship with God.

6 When I at last to heaven ascend
And join that blest abode,
There an eternity I'll spend
In fellowship with God.

145

4s. 3s. & 7s.

HARK! the pealing
Softly stealing,
Funeral bell
Sadly speaks a soul's farewell.

2 Welcome, welcome,
Is thy music
Silvery bell,
Thou hast tolled a saint's farewell.

3 Sweetly sleeping,
Friends why weeping?

"All is well,"
Tolls the solemn funeral bell.

4 Happy hour,
When God's power
Fills the breast;
Sweetly soothing souls to rest.

5 Time is fleeting,
Hearts now beating,
Funeral bell,
Soon will bid the world farewell.

6 Of our number
All will slumber!
Solemn bell,
Thou mayst toll our last farewell.

146 P. M.

WHEN for the eternal world I steer,
And seas are calm, the skies are clear,
And faith in lively exercise,
And distant hills of Canaan rise,
My soul—for joy she claps her wings,
And loud her lovely sonnet sings—
Vain world adieu.

2 With cheerful hopes my eyes explore
Each landmark on the distant shore.
The trees of life and pastures green,
The golden streets and crystal streams,
Again for joy she claps her wings,
And loud her lovely sonnet sings,
Vain world adieu.

3 The nearer still she draws to land,
More eager all her powers expand;
With steady helm and free bent sail,
Her anchor drops within the vale.
Again for joy she claps her wings,
And her celestial sonnet sings—
Glory to God!

147

C. M.

O TELL me where the dove is flown
To build her downy nest,
And I will search the world around,
To win her to my breast.

2 I sought her in the rosy bower
Where pleasure holds her reign;
Where fancy flies from flower to flower,
But there I sought in vain.

3 I sought her in the bower of love,
I knew her tender heart;
But she had flown—that peaceful dove
Had felt the traitor's dart.

4 Upon ambition's craggy hill
I thought this bird might stray,
And there I sought, but vainly still;
She never flew that way.

5 Faith smiled and shed the tender tear
To see me search around,
And whispered "I can tell thee where
The dove may yet be found.

6 In meek religion's humble cot,
She built her downy nest;
Go, seek that sweet secluded spot,
And win her to thy breast."

148 C. M.

YE burden'd souls, to Jesus come;
You need not be afraid;
He loves to hear poor sinners cry,
He loves to hear them plead.

2 Ye humble souls, to Jesus come,
'T was he who made you see
Your wretched, ruin'd, helpless state—
Your guilt and misery.

3 Christ is a friend to mourning souls;
Then why should you despair,
Since Saul and Mary Magdalene
Found grace and mercy here?

149 7s.

CHILDREN of the heavenly King,
As ye journey, sweetly sing;
Sing your Savior's worthy praise,
Glorious in his works and ways.

2 Ye are travelling home to God,
In the way the fathers trod:
They are happy now, and ye
Soon their happiness shall see.

3 O, ye banished seed, be glad!
Christ our advocate is made—
Us to save our flesh assumes:
Brother to our soul becomes.

4 Shout, ye little flock, and blest!
You on Jesus' throne shall rest;
There your seat is now prepar'd,
There your kingdom and reward.

5 Fear not, brethren, joyful stand,
On the borders of your land;
Jesus Christ, your Father's Son,
Bids you undismay'd go on.

6 Lord, submissive make us go,
Gladly leaving all below;
Only thou our Leader be,
And we still will follow thee.

150

7s. & 6s.

I ONCE enjoyed my Lord,
Lived happy in his love,
Delighted in his holy word,
And sought my rest above.

2 This world I did despise,
With all its gaudy show;
Thro' faith in Christ turn'd off mine eyes
From vanities below.

3 I then could praise the Lord,
For his redeeming love,—

I knew his grace did peace afford,
  For I that peace did prove.

4 But oh! alas, my soul!
  Where is my comfort now!
Why did I let my love grow cold,
  And why to idols bow?

5 Trembling to Christ I'll fly,
  And all my sins confess;
Beneath his cross I'll humbly fall,
  And ask restoring grace.

6 I'll mortify my pride,
  Myself I will deny,
And if I perish, Lord, at last,
  Beneath thy cross I'll die.

151 *The Cross.*

MUST Simon bear his cross alone,
  And all the world go free?
No, there's a cross for every one,
  And there's a cross for me.
Yes, there's a cross on Calvary!
Through which by faith the crown I see;
  For me 'tis pardon bringing,
    O, that's the cross for me,
    O, that's the cross for me,
    O, that's the cross for me.

2 How happy are the saints above,
  Who once went mourning here,—
But now they taste unmingled love,
  And joy without a tear;

Yes, perfect love will dry the tear,
And cast out all tormenting fear,
Which round my heart is clinging,
O, that's the love for me, &c.

3 We'll bear the consecrated cross,
Till from the cross we are free,
And then go home to wear the crown,
For there's a crown for me;
Yes, there's a crown in heaven above,
The purchase of a Savior's love,
For me at his appearing;
O, that's the crown for me, &c.

152 *The Happy Land.*

THERE is a happy land, Far, far away,
Where saints in glory stand, Bright, bright as day;
O how they sweetly sing, Worthy is our Savior King,
Loud let his praises ring, Praise, praise, for aye.

2 Come to that happy land, Come, come away;
Why will ye doubting stand, Why still delay;
Oh, we shall happy be, When from sin and sorrow free;
Lord, we shall live with thee, Blest, blest for aye.

3 Bright in that happy land, Beams every eye,
Kept by a father's hand, Love cannot die,
Oh, then, to glory run; Be a crown and kingdom won;
And bright, above the sun, We reign for aye.

4 Now in our youthful days, Come let us sing;
High let our voices raise, Praise to our King;
Angels above the sky, Holy, holy, holy cry,
To God enthroned on high, Jesus their King.

5 There, in that world of light, We all shall meet,
Rob'd in pure raiment white, Each other greet;
Loud then we'll raise the strain To the Lamb that once was slain,
High on the heavenly plain, At Jesus' feet.

153

WILL you come to the cross I have died on for you,
To save you from death, which was justly your due?
Say, will you—will you—will you—will you come to the cross?

2 And while at my feet in contrition you lie,
I'll hush with my love every penitent sigh.
Say, will you—will you—will you—will you take up the cross?

3 'T is your Savior that calls, 't is your God that implores
You sinners to turn and be sinners no more.
Say, will you—will you—will you—will you turn and be free?

4 Be free from the world, its temptation and care,
And take up the cross! it is easy to bear.
Say, will you—will you—will you—will you take up the cross?

5 'T will be feet for the lame, and support for the frail,
And a weapon of war, when thy foes shall assail.
Say, will you—will you—will you—will you take up the cross?

6 I've a mansion prepared for the poor and distress'd,
Where the thief enters not and the weary find rest.
Say, will you—will you—will you—will you dwell with me there?

7 Sinner, take up the cross: in that heavenly land
I've a crown for thy head, and a palm for thy hand,
Say, will you—will you—will you—will you reign
with me there?

154

8s. 5s. 7s. & 4s.

I HAVE sought round the verdant earth,
For unfading joy,
I have tried every source of mirth,
But all, all will cloy;
Lord bestow on me,
Grace to set the spirit free,
Thine the praise shall be,
Mine, mine the joy.

2 I have wandered in mazes dark,
Of doubt and distress,
I have not had a kindling spark.
My spirit to bless;
Cheerless unbelief,
Filled my laboring soul with grief;
What shall give relief?
What shall give peace?

3 I then turned to thy Gospel, Lord,
From folly away,
I then trusted thy holy word,
That taught me to pray;
Here I found release,
Weary spirit here found rest,
Hope of endless bliss,
Eternal day.

4 I will praise now, my heavenly king,
I'll praise and adore;

The heart's richest tribute bring,
To thee, God of power;
And in heaven above,
Saved by thy redeeming love,
Loud the strains shall move,
Forevermore.

155

WE'RE trav'ling home to heaven above—Will you go? Will you go?
To sing the Savior's dying love—Will you go? Will you go?
Millions have reached this blest abode,
Anointed kings and priests to God.
And millions now are on the road,—Will you go? Will you go?

2 We're going to see the bleeding Lamb,—Will you go? Will you go?
In rapt'rous strains to praise his name,—Will you go? Will you go?
The crown of life we there shall wear,
The conqueror's palms our hands shall bear,
And all the joys of Heaven we'll share? Will you go? Will you go?

3 We're going to join the Heavenly Choir,—Will you go? Will you go?
To raise our voice and tune the lyre,—Will you go? Will you go?
There saints and angels gladly sing,
Hosannah to their God and King,
And make the heavenly arches ring,—Will you go? Will you go?

4 Ye weary, heavy laden come—Will you go? Will you go?
In the blest house there still is room,—Will you go? Will you go?

The Lord is waiting to receive,
If thou wilt on him now believe,
He'll give thy troubled conscience ease,—Come believe, O believe!

5 The way to heaven is free for all,—Will you go? Will you go?
For Jew and Gentile—great and small,—Will you go? Will you go?
Make up your mind, give God your heart,
With every sin and idol part,
And now for glory make a start,—Come away! Come away!

156 L. M.

A POOR wayfaring man of grief
Hath often crossed me on my way,
Who sued so humbly for relief,
That I could never answer "nay:"
I had not power to ask his name,
Whither he went or whence he came,
Yet there was something in his eye
That won my love, I knew not why.

2 Once, when my scanty meal was spread,
He entered; not a word he spake;
Just perishing for want of bread;
I gave him all: he blessed it, brake,
And ate,—but gave me part again.
Mine was an angel's portion then,
For while I fed with eager haste,
The crust was manna to my taste.

3 I spied him where a fountain burst
Clear from the rock; his strength was gone;

The heedless water mocked his thirst,
He heard it, saw it hurrying on!
I ran to raise the sufferer up;
Thrice from the stream he drained my cup,
Dipt, and returned it running o'er;
I drank, and never thirsted more.

4 'Twas night; the floods were out; it blew
A winter hurricane aloof;
I heard his voice abroad, and flew
To bid him welcome to my roof;
I warmed, I clothed, I cheered my guest,
Laid him on my own couch to rest;
Then made the hearth my bed, and seemed
In Eden's garden while I dreamed.

5 Stript, wounded, beaten, nigh to death,
I found him by the high way-side;
I roused his pulse, brought back his breath,
Revived his spirit and supplied
Wine, oil, refreshment; he was healed;
I had myself a wound concealed;
But from that hour forgot the smart,
And peace bound up my broken heart.

6 In prison I saw him next condemned
To meet a traitor's doom at morn;
The tide of lying tongues I stemmed,
And honored him midst shame and scorn;
My friendship's utmost zeal to try,
He asked if I for him would die;
The flesh was weak, my blood ran chill,
But the free spirit cried "I will."

7 Then, in a moment, to my view,
The stranger darted from disguise;
The tokens in his hands I knew,
My Savior stood before mine eyes:
He spake; and my poor name he named;
"Of me thou hast not been ashamed:"
These deeds shall thy memorial be;
Fear not, thou didst them unto me.

157 7s. & 5s. Double.

ROUSE ye at the Savior's call!
Sinners, rouse ye one and all;
Wake! or soon your souls will fall,
Fall in deep despair.
Wo to him who turns away,
Jesus kindly calls to-day;
Come, O sinner, while you may,
Raise your soul in prayer.

2 Heard ye not the Savior cry,
"Turn, O turn, why will you die!"
And in keenest agony,
Mourn too late your doom!
Haste, for time is rushing on!
Soon the fleeting hour is gone,
The lifted arrow flies anon,
To sink you in the tomb!

3 By the Savior's bleeding love,
By the joys of heaven above,
Let these words your spirits move;
Quick to Jesus fly!
Come and save your souls from death,
Haste! escape Jehovah's wrath,

Fly! for life's a fleeting breath,
Soon, O soon you'll die.

158 C. M.

O LAND of rest, for thee I sigh,
When will the moments come,
When I shall lay my armor by
And dwell with Christ at home?

2 No tranquil joys on earth I know,
No peaceful sheltering dome;
This world's a wilderness of wo,
This world is not my home.

3 To Jesus Christ I sought for rest,
He bade me cease to roam,
And fly for succor to his breast,
And he'd conduct me home.

4 I should at once have quit the field,
Where foes in fury roam,
But ah, my passport was not sealed,
I could not yet go home.

5 When by affliction sharply tried,
I viewed the gaping tomb,
Although I dread death's chilling tide,
Yet still I sighed for home.

6 Weary of wandering round and round
This vale of sin and gloom,
I long to leave the unhallowed ground,
And dwell with Christ at home.

159

C. M.

LORD! in the morning thou shalt hear
My voice ascending high:
To thee will I direct my prayer,
To thee lift up mine eye.

2 Then to thine house will I resort,
To taste thy mercies there;
I will frequent thy holy court,
And worship in thy fear.

3 Thou art a God before whose sight,
The wicked shall not stand;
Sinners shall ne'er be thy delight,
Nor dwell at thy right hand.

4 But they who love and fear thy name,
Shall see their hopes fulfilled;
The mighty God will compass them
With favor as a shield.

5 O may thy spirit guide my feet
In ways of truth and grace;
Make every path of duty straight,
And plain before my face.

160

TOGETHER let us sweetly live,
I am bound for the land of Canaan;
Together let us sweetly die,
I am bound for the land of Canaan.

CHORUS.

O Canaan, bright Canaan,
I am bound for the land of Canaan:
O Canaan, it is my happy home,
I am bound for the land of Canaan.

2 If you get there before I do,
I am bound for the land of Canaan;
Look out for me, I'm coming too,
I am bound for the land of Canaan.

3 I have some friends before me gone,
I am bound for the land of Canaan;
And I'm resolv'd to travel on,
I am bound for the land of Canaan.

4 Our songs of praise shall fill the skies,
I am bound for the land of Canaan;
While higher still our joys they rise,
I am bound for the land of Canaan.

5 Then come with me, beloved friend,
I am bound for the land of Canaan;
The joys of heaven shall never end,
I am bound for the land of Canaan.

161

WHAT'S this that steals upon my frame—
Is it death? Is it death?
Which soon will quench this vital flame,
Is it death? Is it death?
If this be death, I soon shall be
From every pain and sorrow free—
I shall the King of glory see—
All is well—All is well.

2 Weep not, my friends, weep not for me—
All is well—All is well.
My sins are pardoned, I am free—
All is well—All is well.
There's not a cloud that doth arise
To hide my Jesus from my eyes,
I soon shall mount the upper skies—
All is well—All is well.

3 Tune, tune your harps, ye saints in glory—
All is well—All is well.
I will rehearse the pleasing story—
All is well—All is well.
Bright angels are from glory come,
They're round my bed, and in my room,
They wait to waft my spirit home—
All is well—All is well.

4 Hark! Hark! my Lord and Master calls me—
All is well—All is well.
I soon shall see his face in glory—
All is well—All is well.
Farewell, my friends, adieu, adieu,
I can no longer stay with you,
My glittering crown appears in view—
All is well—All is well.

5 Hail! Hail! all hail, ye blood-washed throng—
Saved by grace—Saved by grace.
I've come to join your rapturous song.
Saved by grace—Saved by grace.
All, all is peace and joy divine,
And heaven and glory now are mine,
Forever with the blest to shine—
All is well—All is well.

162

WHERE is now a righteous Noah?
Where is now a righteous Noah?
Where is now a righteous Noah?
Safe in the promis'd land,

He went up through a flood of water,
He went up through a flood of water,
He went up through a flood of water,
Safe in the promis'd land.

CHORUS.

By and by we do hope to meet him,
By and by we do hope to meet him,
By and by we do hope to meet him,
Safe in the promis'd land.

2 Where is now good old Elijah, &c.
He went up both soul and body, &c.

3 Where are now the ancient worthies, &c.
They went up through a fiery furnace, &c.

4 Where is now a praying Daniel, &c.
He went up through a den of lions, &c.

5 Where is now a Paul and Silas, &c.
They went up through tribulation, &c.

163 P. M.

HOW happy is the man who has chosen wisdom's ways,
And measured out his span to his God in prayer and praise;
His God and his Bible are all that he desires,
To holiness of heart he continually aspires,
In poverty he's happy, for he knows he has a Friend,
Who never will forsake him till the world shall have an end.

2 He rises in the morning, with the lark he tunes his lays,
And offers up his tribute to his God in prayer and praise:

And then to his labors he cheerfully repairs,
In confidence believing that God will hear his pray-
ers,
Whatever he engages in at home or abroad,
His object is to honor and to glorify his God.

3 In sickness, pain and sorrow he never will repine,
While he is drawing nourishmeht from Christ the
living vine.
When trouble presses heavily he leans on Jesus'
breast,
And in his precious promises he finds a quiet rest.
The yoke of Christ is easy, and his burden always
light,
He lives, nor is he weary till Canaan heaves in
sight.

4 'T is thus you have his history through life from day
to day,
Religion is no mystery, with him 't is a beaten way;
And when upon his pillow he lies down to die,
In hope he rejoices for he knows his God is nigh.
And when life's lamp is flickering, his soul on wings
of love,
Flies away to realms of glory, there to reign with
Christ above.

5 And now his spirit's happy, for he's gained the holy
land,
With a crown of glory on his head and palm in his
hand,
With saints, priests and prophets, he'll sweep the
golden lyre,
And shout loud hallelujahs with all the heavenly
choir.
He's happy, in eternity his joy will be complete,
With angels now he's bowing round his glorious
Savior's feet.

164

L. M.

WHEN converts first begin to sing,
Their happy souls are on the wing,

Their theme is all redeeming love,
Fain would they be with Christ above.

With admiration they behold,
The love of Christ that can't be told,
They view themselves upon the shore,
And think the battle all is o'er.

They feel themselves quite free from pain
And think their enemies are slain;
They make no doubt but all is well,
And Satan is cast down to hell.

They wonder why old saints don't sing
And make the heavenly arches ring;
Ring with melodious, joyful sound,
Because a prodigal is found.

Come take up arms and face the field,
Come gird on harness, sword and shield,
Stand fast in faith, fight for your King,
And soon the vict'ry you shall win.

When satan comes to tempt your minds,
Then meet him with these blessed lines—
Jesus our Lord hath swept the field,
And we're determined not to yield.

165

8s.

WHEN Joseph his brethren beheld,
Afflicted and trembling with fear,
His heart with compassion was fill'd,
From weeping he could not forbear.

2 Awhile his behavior was rough,
To bring their past sins to their mind:
But when they were humbled enough,
He hastened to show himself kind.

3 How little they thought it was he,
Whom they had ill treated and sold!
How great their confusion must be,
As soon as his name he had told!

4 "I am Joseph, your brother," he said,
"And still to my heart you are dear;
You sold me and thought I was dead,
But God, for your sakes, sent me here."

5 Though greatly distressed before,
When charged with purloining the cup,
They now were confounded much more,
Not one of them durst look up.

6 Can Joseph whom we would have slain,
Forgive us the evil we did?
And will he our household maintain?
O, this is a brother indeed!

7 Thus dragg'd by my conscience I came,
When laden with guilt to the Lord,
Surrounded with terror and shame,
Unable to utter a word.

8 At first he looked stern and severe;
What anguish then pierced my heart!
Expecting each moment to hear
The sentence—Thou cursed, depart!

9 But oh! what surprise when he spoke—
While tenderness beam'd in his face—
My heart then to pieces was broke,
O'erwhelm'd and confounded by grace.

166 C. M.

AFFLICTIONS though they seem severe,
In mercy oft are sent;
They stop'd the prodigal's career,
And caused him to repent.

CHORUS.

I die with hunger here, he cries,
I starve in foreign lands;
My Father's house has large supplies,
And bounteous are his hands.

2 What have I gained by sin, he said,
But hunger, shame, and fear?
My Father's house abounds with bread,
While I am starving here.

3 I'll go and tell him all I've done,
Fall down before his face;
Unworthy to be called his son,
I'll seek a servant's place.

4 His Father saw him coming back,
He saw, and ran, and smil'd,
And threw his arms around the neck
Of his rebellious child.

5 Father, I've sinned, but O forgive!
Enough, the Father said;

Rejoice my house, my son's alive,
For whom I mourned as dead.

167 L. M.

ETERNITY is just at hand!
And shall I waste my ebbing sand,
And careless view departing day,
And throw my inch of time away?

2 But an eternity there is,
Of endless wo or endless bliss;
And, swift as time fulfils its round,
We to eternity are bound.

3 What countless millions of mankind
Have left this fleeting world behind!
They're gone! but where?—ah, pause and see;
Gone to a long eternity.

4 Sinner, canst thou for ever dwell
In all the fiery deeps of hell?
And is death nothing then to thee;
Death and a dread eternity?

168 P. M.

HEARKEN, ye sprightly, and attend, ye vain ones,
Pause in your mirth, adversity consider;
Learn from a friend's pen, sentimental, painful,
Sick-bed reflections.

2 Healthful and gay, like you I spent my moments,
Fondly my heart said, joy shall last forever;

But I'd forgotten man has no enjoyments,
But by permission.

3 Sudden and awful from the height of pleasure,
By pain and sickness thrown upon a death-bed;
Vain is its softness to assuage the pain of
Raging disorder.

4 Ah! many years I've spent without considering
Man was a mortal, dependent on a moment;
Life but a shadow, time a flying arrow,
Quick to dispel it.

5 Oft have I listen'd while death bells were tolling,
Seen the graves open with spectators mourning,
But was myself, in spite of all these warnings,
Long life expecting.

6 Counsels I've slighted, warnings I've neglected,
In my gay moments, thoughts of death I've banish'd,
When grown grey-headed, often I've resolved
Death to prepare for.

7 Tortured in body, and condemned in spirit,
No sweet composure to direct one prayer,
All is disorder! yet my state eternal
Now is depending.

8 O, ghastly death! pray stop one moment longer,
While I give warning to my gay companions!
No time is granted for expostulation;
Shun my example.

169 11s.

WHILE nature was smiling in stillness to rest,
And the last beams of daylight were dim in the west;
O'er fields by pale moonlight in lonely retreat,
In deep meditation I wandered my feet.

2 I passed a garden—I paused to hear
A voice faint and fault'ring from one kneeling there;
The voice of the mourner affected my heart,
While pleading in anguish the poor sinner's part.

3 I listened a moment, then turned me to see
What man of compassion this stranger could be,
When lo ! I discovered, knelt on the cold ground,
The loveliest being that ever was found.

4 So deep was his sorrow, so fervent his prayer,
That down o'er his bosom rolled sweat, blood and tears!
I wept to behold him, and asked his name,
He answered, 'T is JESUS ! from heaven I came,

5 I am thy redeemer—for thee I must die,
The cup is most bitter, but cannot pass by ;
Thy sins which are many, are laid upon me,
And all this sore anguish I suffer for thee !

6 I heard with attention, the tale of his wo,
While tears of repentance like rivers did flow ;
The cause of his sorrow, to hear him repeat,
Affected my heart, and I fell at his feet :

7 With a voice of contrition I loudly did cry,
Lord, save, or I perish—O, save, or I die !
He smiled when he saw me, and said to me, live !
Thy sins, which are many, I freely forgive !

8 How sweet was that sentence, which made me rejoice !
His looks how consoling ! how charming his voice !
I ran from the garden to spread it abroad,
And shouted hosannah—O glory to God !

170 P. M.

LOW down in this beautiful valley,
Where love crowns the meek and the lowly,

Where loud storms of envy and folly
May roll on their billows in vain.

2 This low vale is far from contention,
There 's no soul can dream of dissension,
No dark wiles of evil invention,
Can find out these regions of peace.

3 The low soul in humble subjection,
Shall there find unshaken protection;
The soft gales of cheering reflection,
The mind soothes in sorrow and pain.

4 O there, there the Lord will deliver,
And souls drink this beautiful river,
Which flows peace forever and ever,
Where love and joy will always increase.

171 L. M.

HAIL, heavenly love that first began
The scheme to rescue fallen man;
Hail, matchless, free, eternal grace,
That gave my soul a hiding place.

2 Against the God who rules the sky,
I fought with hands uplifted high;
Despised the offers of his grace,
Too proud to seek a hiding place.

3 Enwrapp'd in dark Egyptian night,
And fond of darkness more than light,
Madly I ran the sinful race,
Secure without a hiding place.

4 But lo! the eternal counsel ran,
Almighty love arrest the man.
I felt the arrows of distress,
And found I had no hiding place.

5 Eternal justice stood in view,
To Sinai's fiery mount I flew;
But justice cried with frowning face,
This mountain is no hiding place.

6 But lo! a heavenly voice I heard,
And mercy to my soul appear'd;
She led me on a pleasing pace
To Jesus Christ my hiding place.

7 Should storms of sevenfold thunder roll,
And shake the globe from pole to pole,
No thunderbolt would daunt my face,
For Jesus is my hiding place.

8 A few more rolling suns at most,
Will land me safe on Canaan's coast;
Where I shall sing the song of grace,
Safe in my glorious hiding place.

172 L. M.

THERE is an hour divinely blest,
Where earth-born cares are hushed to rest,
When angel spirits hover near,—
It is the holy hour of prayer.

2 There is a place my soul loves well,
Where holy thoughts the bosom swell;
There I can oft alone repair,
It is the place of secret prayer.

3 There is a time to me most sweet,
When friend with friend can gently meet;
'T is round the sacred altar, where
The lov'd of home unite in prayer.

4 There is a sweet, a lovely spot,
Where all our toils are oft forgot;
And friends and foes assemble there,
'T is in the house of social prayer.

5 And often too I fain would go,
Where all may meet while here below;
The rich, the poor, the young and fair,
'T is in the house of public prayer.

6 But there 's a place of heavenly rest,
Where saints, departed, all are blest.
Dear Jesus, may this be my prayer,
That I may dwell forever there.

173 C. M.

NOW is the time, th' accepted hour,
O sinners! come away:
The Savior's knocking at your door,
Arise without delay.

2 Do not refuse to give him room,
Lest mercy should withdraw;

He'll then in robes of vengeance come,
To execute his law.

3 Then where, poor sinners, will you be,
If destitute of grace ;
When you your injured Judge shall see,
And stand before his face ?

4 Let not these warnings be in vain,
But lend a list'ning ear,
Lest you should meet them all again,
When wrapped in keen keen despair.

174 P. M.

THE glorious light of Zion is spreading far and wide,
And sinners now are coming into the gospel tide,
The standard of King Jesus doth now in triumph rise,
And sinners crowd around it, with bitter shrieks and cries.

2 The suff'rings of the Savior upon mount Calvary,
Are sounding sweet to sinners, come this will set you free!
And while this glorious message is circulating round,
Some souls exposed to ruin, redeeming love have found.

3 And of that happy number, I hope that I am one,
And Jesus Christ will finish the work he has begun;
He'll cut it short in righteousness, and I'll forever be,
A monument of mercy in all eternity.

4 I am but a young convert, I lately did enlist,
A soldier under Jesus, my Captain, King and Priest.

I have received my bounty, likewise my martial dress,
A ring of love and favor, a robe of righteousness.

5 And down into the water young converts love to go,
To serve our Lord and Master in righteous acts below;
To lay our sinful bodies beneath the yielding wave;
An emblem of the Savior, when he lay in the grave.

6 Poor sinners, think what Jesus has done for you and me,
Behold his bleeding body suspended on the tree!
His bleeding head, his hands, his side, he doth to you display;
Come tell me, fellow sinner, how can you stay away!

7 Come all ye elder brethren, who're soldiers of the cross,
Who for the sake of Jesus have counted all things dross,
Come pray for us young converts, that we may travel on,
And meet you all in glory, where our Redeemer's gone.

175

8s. & 7s.

COME, ye converts, come and welcome;
All the saints are saying, come;
Joyfully we now receive you
To the church your future home;
Come and welcome, come and welcome,
In our hearts there yet is room.

2 Stay no longer, stay no longer,
From your blessed Savior's fold;
Come, dear youth, ye lambs of Jesus,
He himself hath bid you come;

With his people, with his people,
Join yourselves, and be at home.

3 Now accept the pledge we give you,
While our hands with yours we join,
While our hearts unite together
In the bonds of love divine;
Blessed Jesus, blessed Jesus,
May we all henceforth be thine.

4 Now the vows of God are on you—
Be the slaves of sin no more;
O be humble, holy, faithful,
Till the toils of life are o'er;
Then, dear brethren, then, dear sisters,
May we meet on Canaan's shore.

176 L. M.

PRAYER is appointed to convey,
The blessings God designs to give;
Long as they live should Christians pray,
For only while they pray they live.

2 If pain afflict, or wrongs oppress,
If cares distract, or fears dismay,
If guilt deject, if sin distress,
The remedy's before thee—pray.

3 'T is prayer supports the soul that 's weak:
Though thought be broken, language lame,
Pray, if thou canst, or canst not speak;
But pray with faith in Jesus' name.

177 12s.

THE voice of Free Grace cries escape to the mountain;
For Adam's lost race Christ has opened a fountain:
For sin, and uncleanness, and every transgression,
His blood flows most freely in streams of salvation.
Hallelujah to the Lamb, who hath purchased our pardon;
We'll praise him again when we pass over Jordan.

2 Ye souls that are wounded, O, flee to the Savior;
He calls you in mercy;—'tis infinite favor;
Your sins are increasing; escape to the mountain;
His blood can remove them, which flows from the fountain.
Hallelujah to the Lamb, &c.

3 O Jesus, ride on, triumphantly glorious;
O'er sin, death and hell, thou art more than victorious;
Thy name is the theme of the great congregation,
While angels and men raise the shout of salvation—
Hallelujah to the Lamb, &c.

178 C. P. M.

AS near to Calvary I pass,
Methinks I see a bloody cross,
Where a poor victim hangs;
His flesh with rugged irons tore,
His limbs all dress'd in purple gore,
Gasping in dying pangs.

2 Surpris'd the spectacle to see,
I ask'd, who can this victim be
In such exquisite pain?

Why thus consign'd to woes, I cried?
"'T is I," the bleeding Son replied,
"To save the world from sin."

3 Jesus for rebel mortals dies!
How can it be? my soul replies,
What! Jesus die for me?
"Yes," saith the suffering Son of God,
"I give my life, I spill my blood,
For thee, poor soul, for thee."

4 Lord, since thy life thou'st freely giv'n
To bring my wretched soul to heav'n,
And bless me with thy love,
Then at thy feet, O God, I'll fall,
Give thee my life, my soul, my all,
To reign with thee above.

179

8s. & 7s.

LET thy kingdom, blessed Savior,
Come and bid our jarrings cease;
Come, O come, and reign forever,
God of love, and prince of peace:
Visit now thy precious Zion,
Hear thy people mourn and weep,
Day and night thy lambs are crying,
Come, good Shepherd, feed thy sheep.

2 Some for Paul, some for Apollos,
Some for Cephas—none agree;
Jesus, let us hear thee call us,
Help us, Lord, to follow thee.
Then we 'll rush through what encumbers,
Over every hind'rance leap,

Undismay'd by force or numbers:
  Come, good Shepherd, feed thy sheep.

3 Lord, in us there is no merit,
  We've been sinners from our youth,
Guide us, Lord, by thy good Spirit,
  Which shall teach us all the truth.
On the gospel word we'll venture,
  Till in death's cold arms we sleep,
Love 's our bound and Christ our centre,
  O, good Shepherd, feed thy sheep.

4 Come, good Lord, with courage arm us,
  Persecution rages here,
Nothing, Lord, we know, can harm us,
  While our Shepherd is so near;
Glory, glory, be to Jesus,
  At his name our hearts do leap:
He both comforts us and frees us,
  The good Shepherd feeds his sheep.

5 Hear the Prince of your salvation,
  Saying, "Fear not little flock;
I myself am your foundation,
  You are built upon this rock;
Shun the path of vice and folly,
  Scale the mount although 't is steep;
Look to me and be ye holy,
  I delight to feed my sheep."

6 Christ alone whose merit saves us,
  Taught by him we'll own his name.
Sweetest of all names is Jesus,
  How it doth our souls inflame!
Glory, glory, glory, glory,

Give him glory, he will keep;
He will clear the way before us,
The good Shepherd feeds his sheep.

180 C. M.

WHY, O my soul, why weepest thou?
Tell me from whence arise
Those briny tears that often flow,
Those groans that pierce the skies?

2 Is sin the cause of thy complaint,
Or the chastening rod?
Dost thou an evil heart lament,
And mourn an absent God?

3 Lord, let me weep for nought but sin,
And after none but thee;
And then I would, O that I might!
A constant weeper be!

181

WE are on our journey home!
[Repeat.
To the the New Jerusalem—
To meet the Lord in peace;
That Lord will soon appear—
With the New Jerusalem;
All Christians 'll enter in—
To walk its golden streets;
And see the spotless Lamb—
The blessed Lamb of God;
And play on harps of gold
In praises to his name;

Now angels are hovering round—
To bear the saints all home;
To the New Jerusalem.

182

11s.

LIKE a ship see the church through the ocean she rolls:
She 's freighted with grace and well mann'd out with live souls!
Midst whirlwinds and tempests she sails through the world,
While storms of temptation against her are hurl'd.

2 She's bound from the world, through the tempest she flies,
She mounts o'er the billows, is bound for the skies,
While Christ stands at helm no danger she'll fear;
Her captain and pilot knows which way to steer.

3 She stops not to anchor in harbors below,
But o'er life's rough billows her true course doth go,
The highlands of heaven she still keeps in view:
Intends there to anchor and there land her crew.

4 While hell and her legions around her do roar,
Like waves of the ocean which break on the shore;
She steers her course onward, nor heeds the alarm,
With Christ in the vessel, she smiles at the storm.

5 The ebb-tide of nature, which feeds the dead sea,
And the gulf of confusion, together agree
To hinder her progress, her march to oppose;
She spreads forth her canvass and outsails her foes.

6 She 's hated by worldlings, despised by all fools,
Who sail the black sea till they shipwreck their souls!
She kindly invites them their course to bewail,
Yet tarries not for them but spreads the more sail.

7 She's rapidly sailing, with strong gales of love,
And soon will strike soundings on fair coasts above,
Make the highlands of heaven, and enter the road,
And anchor for'er in the kingdom of God.

183

AT life's early morn,
When my Bible was dear,
A voice from its pages
Oft breathed o'er my ear,—
"Oh grieve not the Spirit! Oh grieve not the
Spirit!
Oh grieve not his love.

2 Of my mother I asked,
As I knelt at her knee
To say my sweet prayer,
What was whispering to me?
She answered, "The Spirit! The blest, Holy
Spirit!
Oh grieve not His love."

3 When I mus'd all alone,
And gray twilight was nigh,
While the bright streams of childhood
Went murmuring by,
A voice warned me heavenward! The Voice
of the Spirit,
The Spirit of love.

4 Then youth, with its snares
Did my footsteps entwine,
And I hardened my heart
To that impulse divine—

"Repent!" cried the Spirit, the witnessing
Spirit,
The Spirit of love.

5 But years fled apace,
And with sin I grew wild,
For the world and its tempters
My conscience defiled—
So I slighted the Spirit, the pitying Spirit,
The Spirit of love.

6 And now I am old,
My temples are hoar
And I feel the warm breath
Of His impulse no more,
For I slighted the Spirit—the long waiting
Spirit,
I mocked at His love.

7 Alas! I must die,
And I fear to depart,
Forsaken by Him
Why converteth the heart!
Oh! grieve not the Spirit—the life-giving
Spirit,
The Spirit of love.

184 11s.

HOW sweet in the musing of faith, to repair
To the garden where Mary delighted to rove;
To sit by the tomb where she breathed her fond
prayer,
And paid her sad tribute of sorrow and love,

2 To see the bright beam which disperses her fear,
As the stone is removed from the sepulchre's door,
And the voice of the angel salutes her glad ear,—
"The Savior has risen—he 's a captive no more!"

3 O Savior! as oft as our footsteps we bend
In penitent sadness to weep at thy grave,
On the wings of thy greatness in pity descend,
Be ready to comfort, and mighty to save.

4 We shrink not from scenes of desertion and wo,
If there we may meet with the Lord of our love;
Contented, with Mary, to sorrow below,
If with her we drink of thy fountains above.

185 P. M.

HOW lovely the place where the Savior appears
To those who believe in his word;
His presence disperses my sorrows and fears,
And bids me rejoice in my Lord.

2 One day in his courts, than a thousand beside,
Is better and lovelier far—
My soul hates the tents where the wicked reside,
And all their delights I abhor.

3 Lord, give me a place with the humblest of saints,
For low at thy feet I would lie:
I know that thou hearest my feeble complaints,
Thou hearest the young raven's cry.

4 Give strength to the souls that now wait upon thee,
O! come, in thy chariot of love;
From earth's vain enchantments, O! help us to flee,
And to set our affections above.

186 C. M.

FATHER, what'er of earthly bliss,
Thy sov'reign will denies,

Accepted at thy throne of grace,
Let this petition rise.

2 Give me a calm and thankful heart,
From every murmur free;
The blessings of thy grace impart,
And make me live to thee.

3 Let the sweet hope that thou art mine,
My life and death attend;
Thy presence through my journey shine,
And crown my journey's end.

187 L. M.

TRIUMPHANT Zion! lift thy head
From dust, and darkness and the dead;
Tho' humbled long, awake at length,
And gird thee with thy Savior's strength.

2 Put all thy beauteous garments on,
And let thy excellence be known:
Deck'd in the robes of righteousness,
Thy glory shall the world confess.

3 No more shall foes unclean invade,
To fill thy hallowed walls with dread;
No more shall hell's insulting host
Their victory and thy sorrows boast.

4 God from on high has heard thy prayer;
His hand thy ruins shall repair;
Nor will thy watchful monarch cease
To guard thee in eternal peace.

188

HEAR the royal proclamation,
The glad tidings of salvation;
Offer'd free for every creature,
Of the ruin'd sons of nature!
Jesus reigns!
He reigns victorious,
Over heaven and earth most glorious,
Jesus reigns!

2 'T was for you that Jesus died,
And for you was crucified!
Conquer'd death and rose to heaven,
Life eternal through him given;
Jesus reigns, &c.

3 Turn unto the Lord most holy;
Shun the paths of vice and folly;
Turn, or you are lost forever!
Oh, now fly unto the Savior—
Jesus reigns, &c.

189

8s. 7s. & 4s.

O'ER the gloomy hills of darkness,
Look, my soul—be still and gaze;
See the promises advancing
To a glorious day of grace!
Blessed jubilee;
Let thy glorious morning dawn!

2 Let the dark benighted pagan,
Let the rude barbarian, see

That divine and glorious conquest
Once obtained on Calvary;
Let the gospel
Loud resound, from pole to pole.

3 Kingdoms wide, that sit in darkness,
Grant them, Lord, the glorious light;
Now from eastern coast to western,
May the morning chase the night;
Let redemption,
Freely purchased, win the day!

4 Fly abroad, thou mighty gospel,
Win and conquer—never cease!
May thy lasting, wide dominions
Multiply, and still increase;
Sway thy sceptre,
Savior, all the world around!

190

Air—*God is love.*

THE Lord has called—has called me by his word:
Saying turn, saying turn—
And leave your sins—your sins of one accord—
Saying turn, saying turn.
But I have turned a stubborn ear,
To every call from year to year,
And now must sink in deep despair—
All's not well, all's not well.

2 I've heard the voice of preachers true and kind—
Saying turn, saying turn—
Who oft have wept—have wept for me, & mourn'd,
Saying turn, saying turn.
But all their tears I did despise,
Entreaties, prayers, and solemn cries—
Against the truth I turned my eyes—
All's not well, all's not well

3 Now death has come, has come to stop my breath:
All's not well, all's not well.
I soon must sink beneath the hand of death—
All's not well, all's not well.
Had I but turned at mercy's cry,
And sought salvation when brought nigh,
I might have been prepared to die.
All's not well, all's not well.

4 And now my friends, my friends and neighbors here—
All's not well, all's not well.
Can you but pray, O raise one fervent prayer—
All's not well, all's not well.
My soul is sunk in deep distress,
O pray that God would grant me grace,
That I may leave the world in peace—
All's not well, all's not well.

5 Young people think, O think on wretched me—
All's not well, all's not well.
My dying words—these words you oft may see—
All's not well, all's not well.
Do not despise the Savior now—
But while you may in mercy bow—
Fly, fly from wrath and dreadful wo,
All's not well, all's not well.

191 C. M.

THE Christian has a light to shine
Upon the dismal tomb—
A light of glory, thus divine,
Dispels the darkest gloom.

2 The Christian has a treasure rare,
A crown of glory bright;
Its dazzling rays are brighter far,
Than noonday's brilliant light.

3 The Christian has a harp so sweet—
A harp of purest gold—
Its melodies can well compete
With David's harp of old.

4 The Christian has a rich reward,
Eternal life in heav'n;
'T was bought by Christ's own precious blood,
By Jesus Christ 't is given.

192

C. M.

SAY. brethren dear, why sleep we here,
Or sink into despair;
While sinners go to worlds of wo,
And perish ever there!

2 Come sisters, too, the way pursue
That leads from earth to heaven,
Up Zion's hill march on, until
The promis'd crown is given.

3 Backsliders, too, what will you do
When God your souls shall call?
In that dread day what will you say
To Christ the judge of all?

4 Come sinners, now, to Jesus bow,
His gospel comfort gives;
Pardon he'll give, thy soul shall live,
Beneath his balmy wings.

193

COME old and come young, and hear me relate,
My life and adventures, and my present state.

I pray you all give ear, to what you now shall hear,
And my story will pleasure and sorrow create.

2 My childhood and youth, in vanity I spent,
Regardless of the truth, and to folly intent;
For more than eighteen years, I shed no mourning tears,
But plead for my sins, and refused to repent.

3 Inflexibly hard, impenetrably blind,
The pleasures of sin had blinded my mind;
To me it did appear, God's law was too severe,
To the cross of the gospel, I was not inclin'd.

4 But O! what love, the love of God to man,
That everlasting love, which drew the saving plan;
That love pursued my soul, when it was sick and foul,
And it showed me how near to the brink I did stand.

5 Sin then appeared vile, the law appeared right,
And justice, and truth, and holiness shone bright;
The word of God was true, and lovely in my view,
But the pardon of sin, it was out of my sight.

6 I languish'd and mourn'd, how long I cannot tell,
I saw God was just, if I sunk down to hell;
My heart was dreadful hard, and the door of grace seemed barr'd,
And my soul with the devils, I feared it would dwell.

7 But when all my hopes were nearly fled away,
And hell from beneath seemed gaping for its prey;
Then Jesus did appear to dissipate my fears,
And he took all the load from my conscience away.

8 O what freedom then I felt, what joys did arise:
And glory was open'd and beaming through the skies;
I freely gave up all, and at his feet did fall,
And glory, all glory, to him I did cry.

9 His voice then I heard in sweet majestic sound,
I have sought you, and found you, and healed all your wounds;
I have work for you to do, be faithful, just and true,
And proclaim to the world what a Savior you've found.

194 C. M.

YE heralds of the cross, go forth,
Proclaim the Savior's name:
Go, preach the gospel to the north—
Let south receive the same.

2 To all the world, the tidings bear;
Go sound salvation free;
And in God's kingdom you will share
A joyful victory.

3 Go, tell the sinner of his ways,
Of judgment yet to come;
Tell him hell's waiting for its prey,
And awful is his doom.

4 Fear not the face of mortal clay—
Let none despise thy youth;
Steadfastly walk in wisdom's way,
Obedient to the truth.

195 H. M.

THOUGH youth's delightful bloom
Dwells sweetly on thy cheek,
Soon in the silent tomb
Thy form in death may sleep—

Thy soul in judgment must appear,
And answer for your actions here.

2 Though prospects now are bright,
And pleasures light thy way,
Thy day may turn to night—
Thy earthly hopes decay;
Vain the pursuit of happiness,
Earth can afford no perfect bliss.

3 Ye blooming youth, beware;
From ways of folly flee;
Shun the vile tempter's snare,
While moral agents free.
Listen unto the Savior's voice,
And make the way to heav'n your choice.

4 Jesus was crucified
To save your souls from hell;
For you he bled and died,
That you with him might dwell—
Around his throne forever sing,
And love and praise our heav'nly King.

196 C. M.

MY sins, how num'rous, Lord, they are;
I'll bow before thy throne;
Can I obtain forgiveness there,
If penitent I come?

2 Yes, Lord, I know thou wilt forgive
The broken, contrite heart;
Then let an humble sinner live,
And grace to him impart.

3 Since thou hast died for all mankind,
And hear'st the sinner's prayer,
Say, Lord, must I be left behind,
To perish in despair?

4 Pardon my sins and follies past,
Remove my burden now;
Save thou my soul from hell at last,
And faithfulness I vow.

5 Thy name I ever will adore,
Thou just and holy one;
I'll tread the ways of sin no more,
If thou my name wilt own.

197

8s. & 7s.

SISTER, thou wast mild and lovely,
Gentle as the summer-breeze,
Pleasant as the air of evening,
When it floats among the trees.

2 Peaceful be thy silent slumber.
Peaceful in the grave so low;
Thou no more wilt join our number,
Thou no more our songs shalt know.

3 Dearest sister, thou hast left us,
Here thy loss we deeply feel,
But 't is God that hath bereft us,
He can all our sorrows heal.

4 Yet again we hope to meet thee,
When the day of life is fled,

Then in heaven with joy to greet thee,
  Where no farewell tear is shed.

198 C. M.

BACKSLIDERS, who your misery feel,
  Attend your Savior's call;
Return, he'll your backslidings heal:
  O crown him Lord of all.

2 Though crimson sin increase your guilt,
  And painful is your thrall,
For broken hearts his blood was spilt:
  O crown him Lord of all.

3 Take with you words, approach his throne,
  And low before him fall;
He understands the spirit's groan:
  O crown him Lord of all.

4 Whoever comes he'll not cast out,
  Although your faith be small;
His faithfulness you cannot doubt:
  O crown him Lord of all.

199 8s. & 7s.

YE who know your sins forgiven,
  And are happy in the Lord,
Have you read that precious promise,
  Found recorded in his word.
I'll impart to you my spirit,
  I will cleanse you from all sin,
Sanctify and make you holy,
  I will reign and dwell within.

2 Though you have much peace and comfort,
Greater things you yet may find—
Freedom from unholy tempers,
Freedom from the carnal mind;
To procure this perfect freedom,
Jesus suffered, groaned and died—
On the cross the healing fountain,
Gushed from his bleeding side.

3 Wake up, brethren, wake up, sisters—
Seek, O seek that holy state,
None but holy ones can enter
Through those pure celestial gates,—
Can you bear the thoughts of losing
All the joys that are above?
No, my brethren, no, my sisters,
God will perfect you in love.

200

12s.

THE chariot! the chariot! its wheels roll in fire,
As the Lord cometh down in the pomp of his ire:
Lo! self-moving it drives on its pathway of cloud,
And the heavens with the burden of Godhead are bowed.

2 The glory! the glory! around him array'd,
Mighty hosts of the angels now wait on the Lord;
And the glorified saints, and the martyrs are there,
And there all who the palm-wreaths of victory wear!

3 The trumpet! the trumpet! the dead have all heard:
Lo! the depths of the stone-covered charnel are stirred!
From the sea, from the earth, from the south, from the north,
All the vast generations of men are come forth!

4 The judgment! the judgment! the thrones are all set,
Where the Lamb and the white-vested elders are met!
There all flesh is at once in the sight of the Lord,
And the doom of eternity hangs on his word.

5 In mercy, in mercy, look down from above,
Great Creator, on us, thy sad children, with love!
When beneath to their darkness the wicked are driven,
May our justified souls find a welcome in heaven.

201

12s. & 11s.

HARK, sinner, while God from on high doth entreat thee,
And warnings with accents of mercy doth blend;
Give ear to his voice, lest in judgment he meet thee:
"The harvest is passing, the summer will end."

2 How oft of thy danger and guilt he hath told thee!
How oft still the message of mercy doth send!
Haste, haste, while he waits in his arms to enfold thee;
"The harvest is passing, the summer will end."

3 Despised, rejected, at length he may leave thee:
What anguish and horror thy bosom will rend!
Then haste thee, O sinner, while he will receive thee:
"The harvest is passing, the summer will end."

4 Ere long, and Jehovah will come in his power;
Our God will arise, with his foes to contend;
Haste, haste thee, O sinner; prepare for that hour;
"The harvest is passing, the summer will end."

5 The Savior will call thee in judgment before him:
O, bow to his sceptre, and make him thy Friend;
Now, yield him thy heart, and make haste to adore him;
"The harvest is passing, thy summer will end."

202

L. M.

COME hither, all ye weary souls,
Ye heavy-laden sinners, come;
I'll give you rest from all your toils,
And raise you to my heavenly home.

2 "They shall find rest who learn of me:
I'm of a meek and lowly mind:
But passion rages like the sea,
And pride is restless as the wind.

3 "Blest is the man whose shoulders take
My yoke, and bear it with delight:
My yoke is easy to the neck;
My grace shall make the burden light."

4 Jesus, we come at thy command:
With faith and hope, and humble zeal,
Resign our spirits to thy hand,
To mould and guide us at thy will.

203

11s.

THOU sweet gliding Cedron, by thy silver streams,
Our Savior at midnight when moonlight's pale beams
Shone bright on the waters, would frequently stray,
And lose, in thy murmurs, the toils of the day.

2 How damp were the vapors that fell on his head!
How hard was his pillow,—how humble his bed!
The angels, astonished, grew sad at the sight,
And followed their Master with solemn delight.

3 O Garden of Olives, thou dear honored spot,
The fame of thy wonders shall ne'er be forgot;

The theme most transporting to seraphs above;
The triumph of sorrow,—the triumph of love!

4 Come, saints, and adore him—come, bow at his feet!
O, give him the glory, the praise that is meet;
Let joyful hosannas unceasing arise,
And join the full chorus that gladdens the skies.

204 C. M.

PRAYER is the soul's sincere desire
Unuttered or expressed,
The motion of a hidden fire,
That trembles in the breast.

2 Prayer is the burden of a sigh,
The falling of a tear,
The upward glancing of an eye,
When none but God is near.

3 Prayer is the simplest form of speech
That infant lips can try;
Prayer, the sublimest strains that reach
The Majesty on high.

4 Prayer is the Christian's vital breath,
The Christian's native air,
His watchword at the gates of death;
He enters heaven with prayer.

205 C. M.

PRAYER is the contrite sinner's voice,
Returning from his ways,
While angels in their songs rejoice,
And cry, "Behold he prays."

2 The saints in prayer appear as one
In word, in deed, and mind,
While with the Father and the Son
Sweet fellowship they find.

3 Nor prayer is made on earth alone;
The Holy Spirit pleads,
And Jesus, on th' eternal throne,
For sinners intercedes.

4 O Thou, by whom we come to God,—
The life, the truth, the way,—
The path of prayer thyself hast trod;
Lord, teach us how to pray.

206

7s. & 6s.

GO, when the morning shineth,
Go, when the moon is bright,
Go, when the eve declineth,
Go, in the hush of night;
Go, with pure mind and feeling,
Fling earthly thought away,
And, in thy chamber kneeling,
Do thou in secret pray.

2 Remember all who love thee,
All who are lov'd by thee;
Pray too, for those who hate thee,
If any such there be;
Then for thyself, in meekness,
A blessing humbly claim,
And link with each petition
Thy great Redeemer's name.

3 Or if 't is e'er deni'd thee
In solitude to pray,
Should holy thoughts come o'er thee,
When friends are round thy way;
E'en then the silent breathing,—
Thy spirit rais'd above,—
Will reach his throne of glory,
Who's Mercy, Truth, and Love.

4 Oh! not a joy nor blessing
With this can we compare,
The pow'r that he hath giv'n us
To pour our souls in pray'r!
When'er thou pin'st in sadness
Before his footstool fall,—
Remember, in thy gladness,
His love who gave thee all.

207 C. M.

JESUS, thou art the sinner's friend,
As such I look to thee;
Now in the bowels of thy love,
O Lord, remember me.

2 Remember thy pure word of grace;
Remember Calvary!
Remember all thy dying groans,
And then remember me.

3 Thou wondrous Advocate with God!
I yield myself to thee;
While thou art sitting on thy throne,
O Lord, remember me.

4 I own I'm guilty, own I'm vile,
Yet thy salvation 's free;
Then, in thy all-bounding grace,
O Lord, remember me.

5 How'er forsaken or distress'd,
How'er oppress'd I be,
How'er afflicted here on earth,
Do thou remember me.

6 And when I close my eyes in death,
And creature helps all flee,
Then, O my great Redeemer, God,
I pray remember me.

208

7s.

The Dying Thief.

JESUS Christ has power alone
To subdue a heart of stone;
And the moment grace is felt,
Then the hardest heart will melt.

2 When our Lord was crucified,
Two transgressors with him died;
One, with vile blaspheming tongue,
Scoff'd at Jesus, as he hung.

3 Thus he spent his wicked breath
In the very jaws of death;
Perish'd, as too many do,
With the Savior in his view.

4 But the other, touch'd with grace
Saw the danger of his case;

Faith received to own the Lord,
Whom the scribes and priests abhor'd.

5 Lord, he pray'd, remember me,
When in glory thou shalt be;
Soon with me, the Lord replies,
Thou shalt rest in paradise.

6 This was wondrous grace indeed!
Grace bestow'd in time of need!
Sinners, trust in Jesus' name,
You shall find him still the same.

209 Tune—"*Sweet Home.*"

WHEN torn is the bosom by sorrow or care,
Be it ever so simple, there's nothing like prayer;
It eases, soothes, softens, subdues, yet sustains,
Gives vigor to hope, and puts passion in chains.
Prayer, prayer, O, sweet prayer,
Be it ever so simple, there 's nothing like prayer.

2 When far from the friends we hold dearest we part,
What fond recollections still cling to the heart,
Past converse, past scenes, past enjoyments are there,
Oh how hurtfully pleasing till hallowed by prayer.
Prayer, prayer, O, sweet prayer,
Be it ever so simple, there 's nothing like prayer.

3 When pleasure would woo us from piety's arms,
The siren sings sweetly, or silently charms,
We listen, love, loiter, are caught in the snare,
On looking to Jesus we conquer by prayer.
Prayer, prayer, O, sweet prayer,
Be it ever so simple, there 's nothing like prayer.

4 While strangers to prayer, we are strangers to bliss,

Heaven pours its full streams thro' no medium but
this,
And till we the seraph's full ecstacy share,
Our chalice of joy must be guarded by prayer.
Prayer, prayer, O, sweet prayer,
Be it ever so simple, there's nothing like prayer.

210

11s.

"Remember Lot's Wife."

HOW prone are professors to rest on their lees,
To study their pleasure, their profit and ease;
Though God says, Arise, and escape for thy life,
And look not behind thee,—Remember Lot's wife.

2 Awake from thy slumbers, the warning believe;
'T is Jesus that calls thee, the message receive;
While dangers are pending, escape for thy life,
And look not behind thee,—Remember Lot's wife.

3 How many poor souls has the tempter beguiled,
With specious temptations how many defiled!
O be not deluded, escape for thy life,
And look not behind thee,—Remember Lot's wife.

4 The ways of religion true pleasure afford,
No pleasures can equal the joys of the Lord:
Forsake then the world, and escape for thy life,
And look not behind thee,—Remember Lot's wife.

5 But if you determine the call to refuse,
And venture the way of destruction to choose;
For hell you will part with the blessings of life,
And then, if not now, you'll remember Lot's wife.

211

12s. & 11s.

THOU art gone to the grave; but we will not de
plore thee,
Though sorrows and darkness encompass the
tomb;

The Savior has passed through its portals before thee,
And the lamp of his love is thy guide through the gloom.

2 Thou art gone to the grave; we no longer behold thee,
Nor tread the rough paths of the world by thy side;
But his wide arms of mercy are spread to enfold thee,
And sinners may hope, since the Savior hath died.

3 Thou art gone to the grave; and, its mansions forsaking,
Perhaps thy weak spirit in doubt lingered long;
But the sunshine of heaven beamed bright on thy waking,
And the sound thou didst hear was the seraphim's song.

4 Thou art gone to the grave; but we will not deplore thee,
Since God was thy Ransom, thy Guardian, thy Guide;
He gave thee, he took thee, and he will restore thee;
And death has no sting, since the Savior hath died.

212 L. M.

I LONG to see the season come
When sinners shall come flocking home,
To taste the sweets of Jesus' love,
And seek the joys that are above.

2 Hark! how the glorious gospel sounds,
Inviting sinners all around;

Behold your loving Savior stands,
And spreads for you his bleeding hands.

3 Attend, poor sinners, to his word;
Serve him, yea, own him as your Lord.
He'll wash you in atoning blood,
And seal you heirs and sons of God.

4 A few more days and you must go
To realms of joy or endless wo;—
In worlds of light with Christ to dwell,
Or sink beneath his frowns to hell.

5 Come then, dear sinners, counsel take,
And all your sinful ways forsake;
This world give up, leave friends behind,
In Christ you shall redemption find.

6 Take your companion by the hand,
Take all your children in a band;
And give them up at Jesus' call,
To pardon, bless, and save them all.

7 Then when the day of Christ shall come,
And he collects his children home;
On Zion's mount you all shall stand,
And join the bright angelic band.

8 O, what a glorious company!
May I be there the sight to see,
And join in praise to Jesus' name,
All glorious in Jerusalem.

213

HERE o'er the earth as a stranger I roam,
Here is no rest, is no rest;
Here as a pilgrim I wander alone,
Yet I am blest, I am blest;
For I look forward to that glorious day,
When sin and sorrow will vanish away;
My heart doth leap while I hear Jesus say,
There, there is rest, there is rest.

2 Here fierce temptations beset me around;
Here is no rest, is no rest;
Here I am griev'd while my foes me surround:
Yet I am blest, I am blest.
Let them revile me, and scoff at my name,
Laugh at my weeping,—endeavor to shame;
I will go forward, for this is my theme;
There, there is rest, there is rest.

3 Here are afflictions and trials severe;
Here is no rest, is no rest;
Here I must part with the friends I hold dear;
Yet I am blest, I am blest.
Sweet is the promise I read in his word;
Blessed are they who have died in the Lord;
They have been call'd to receive their reward;
There, there is rest, there is rest.

4 This world of cares is a wilderness state,
Here is no rest, is no rest;
Here I must bear from the world all its hate,
Yet I am blest, I am blest.
Soon I shall be from the wicked released,
Soon shall the weary forever be blest;
Soon shall I lean upon Jesus' soft breast;
There, there is rest, there is rest.

214 *Eld. Clement Phinney's Experience.*

I'LL sing a song which doth belong
To all the people round me,
I'll spread the fame of Jesus' name,
And tell how Jesus found me.

2 'T was in distress and wickedness,
These words he spake unto me,
O sinner, come, in me there's room,
O how these words ran through me.

3 I was like Paul, who was call'd Saul,
In bitter persecution;
I did disdain being born again,
And called it all delusion.

4 I fought the saints without restraint,
Too proud to cry for mercy;
Conviction strong did come along,
Oh! how these things did pierce me.

5 I did not know which way to go,
My sins appeared like mountains;
All filled with wo, my tears did flow,
My head was like a fountain.

6 My soul has been so long in sin,
How can I be forgiven?
Then Jesus came, oh! bless his name,
And fill'd my soul with heaven.

7 I rais'd my voice and did rejoice,
Sang glory, glory, glory;

Then I did find Jesus was mine,
Oh! what a pleasing story.

8 Come sinners now, to Jesus bow,
While grace is offered to you;
Come as you are, to Christ repair,
Or sin will sure undo you.

9 With lovely charms and open arms,
Now Jesus will receive you;
Come, sinners, come, in him there's room,
And Jesus will relieve you.

215 "*Hail to the Brightness.*"

HAIL to the brightness of Zion's glad morning!
Joy to the lands that in darkness have lain;
Hush'd be the accents of sorrow and mourning,
Zion in triumph begins her mild reign.

2 Hail to the brightness of Zion's glad morning,
Long by the prophets of Israel foretold;
Hail to the millions from bondage returning,
Gentiles and Jews the blest vision behold.

3 Lo, in the desert rich flowers are springing,
Streams ever copious are gliding along;
Loud from the mountain-tops echoes are ringing
Wastes rise in verdure, and mingle in song.

4 See, the dead risen from land and from ocean,
Praise to Jehovah ascending on high;
Fall'n are the engines of war and commotion,
Shouts of salvation are rending the sky.

216 "*Lead me to the Rock.*"

O SAVIOR of sinners, when faint and depress'd,
With manifold trials and sorrows oppress'd,
I'll bow at thy feet, and with confidence cry,
'Lead me to the rock that is higher than I!'

2 When tempted by Satan the Spirit to grieve—
The service of Christ, my Redeemer to leave,
I'll claim my relation to Jesus on high,
The rock of salvation that's higher than I.

3 When judgments, O Lord, are abroad in the land,
And merited vengeance descends from thy hand!
O'erwhelmed with the sight, for protection I'll fly,
And hide in the Rock, that is higher than I!

4 When summoned away before God to appear,
By free-grace supported I'll yield without fear!
Most gladly I'll venture with Jesus on high,
To enter the Rock that is higher than I.

5 'T is there, with the chosen of Jesus, I long
To dwell, and eternally join in the song,
Of praising and blessing with angels on high,
Christ Jesus, the Rock that is higher than I!

6 The faithful, sure promise the fathers believed,
Shall then be fulfilled and the glory received;
The hand that was pierced for me wipe my tears dry,
For to reign with the One that is higher than I.

217 "*Lord's Prayer.*"

OUR Father who in heaven art,
Hallowed be thy name;
Thy kingdom come, Thy will be done,
In heav'n and earth the same.

CHORUS.

Come my Savior, O my Savior,
Come and bless thy people now,
While at thy feet we humbly bow,
O come and save us now,
Then will we sing our sufferings o'er,
And praise thee evermore;
Then will we sing our suff'rings o'er,
And praise thee evermore.

2 Give us this day our daily bread;
Our trespasses forgive;
As we forgive our fellow men,
May we thy grace receive.
Come, my Savior, &c.

3 And in temptation leave us not;
From evil us defend;
For thine, O Lord, the kingdom is,
For ever, without end.
Come, my Savior, &c.

4 Thine is the power, O Lord, to bring
The kingdom down to men;
Thine is the glory evermore,
And kingdom without end.
Come, my Savior, &c.

5 In that glad day shall all thy saints
A joyful tribute bring,
Of praise and pow'r, of joy and song,
To their exalted king.
Come, my Savior, &c.

218

8s. 7s. & 4s.

SAVIOR, visit thy plantation;
Grant us, Lord, a gracious rain;
All will come to desolation,
Unless thou return again:
Lord, revive us!
All our help must come from thee.

2 Surely once thy garden flourished;
Every part looked gay and green;
All its plants by thee were nourished;
Then how cheering was the scene!
Lord, revive us!
All our help must come from thee.

3 Keep no longer at a distance;
Shine upon us from on high,
Lest, for want of thine assistance,
Every plant should droop and die:
Lord, revive us!
All our help must come from thee.

4 Gracious Savior, hasten hither;
Thou canst make them bloom again;
O, permit them not to wither;
Let not all our hopes be vain:
Lord, revive us!
All our help must come from thee.

5 Let our mutual love be fervent;
Make us prevalent in prayers;
Let each one esteem thy servant,
Shun the world's bewitching snares:

Lord, revive us!
All our help must come from thee.

6 Break the tempter's fatal power,
Turn the stony heart to flesh,
And begin from this good hour,
To revive thy work afresh:
Lord, revive us!
All our help must come from thee.

219

7s.

MIGHTY God, on thee we call,
O look down on Zion's wall;
Build her ruins that are wide,
Lord, appear on Zion's side.

2 See thy people, gracious God,
Scatter'd and dispers'd abroad;
How their foes do them deride,
Lord, appear on Zion's side.

3 Once they sang thy praises bold,
And with joy thy wonders told;
Now they mourn,—in sorrow hide,
Lord, appear on Zion's side.

4 Love is cold and sins abound,
Truth is scarcely to be found;
Error doth in triumph ride,
Lord, appear on Zion's side.

5 Build thy people up again,—
May they evermore remain,

And within thy grace abide;
Lord, appear on Zion's side.

220

10s.

JOYFULLY, joyfully onward I move,
Bound for the land of bright spirits above.
Angelic choristers sing as I come,
Joyfully, joyfully haste to thy home.
Soon, with my pilgrimage ended below,
Home to the land of bright spirits I go,
Pilgrim and stranger no more shall I roam,
Joyfully, joyfully resting at home.

2 Friends fondly cherish'd have pass'd on before,
Waiting, they watch me approaching the shore;
Singing to cheer me through death's chilling gloom,
Joyfully, joyfully haste to thy home.
Sounds of sweet melody fall on my ear,
Harps of the blessed your voices I hear!
Rings with the harmony heaven's high dome,
Joyfully, joyfully haste to thy home.

3 Death, with thy weapons of war lay me low;
Strike, king of terrors, I fear not the blow;
Jesus hath broken the bars of the tomb;
Joyfully, joyfully will I go home.
Bright will the morn of eternity dawn,
Death shall be banish'd, his sceptre be gone;
Joyfully then shall I witness his doom;
Joyfully, joyfully, safely at home.

221

8s. & 4s.

JESUS died on Calvary's mountain,
Long time ago.
And salvation's rolling fountain
Now freely flows.

2 Once his voice in tones of pity,
Melted in wo,
And he wept o'er Judah's city,
Long time ago.

3 On his head the dews of midnight
Fell, long ago;
Now a crown of dazzling sunlight
Sits on his brow.

4 Jesus died—yet lives forever,
No more to die—
Bleeding Jesus, blessed Savior
Now reigns on high.

5 Now in heav'n he's interceding
For dying men;
Soon he'll finish all his pleading
And come again.

6 Budding fig-trees tell that summer
Dawns o'er the land;
Signs portend that Jesus' coming
Is near at hand.

7 Children, let your lights be burning,
In hopes of heav'n,
Waiting for our Lord's returning
At dawn of ev'n.

8 When he comes, a voice from heav'n
Shall pierce the tomb,
"Come, ye blessed of my father;
Children, come home."

222

8s.

FAREWELL, my brethren in the Lord;
The gospel sounds a jubilee;
My stamm'ring tongue shall sound aloud,
From land to land, from sea to sea;
And as I preach from place to place,
I'll trust alone in God's free grace.

2 Farewell, in bonds of union dear,
Like strings you twine about my heart;
I humbly beg your earnest pray'r,
Till we shall meet no more to part;
Till we shall meet in heaven above,
Encircled in eternal love.

3 Farewell, my earthly friends below,
Though all so kind and dear to me;
My Jesus calls, and I must go,
To sound the gospel jubilee;
To sound the joys and bear the news
To Gentiles and the royal Jews.

4 Farewell, young people, one and all;
While God shall give me breath to breathe,
I'll pray to the Eternal ALL,
That your dear souls in Christ may live;
That your dear souls prepar'd may be
To dwell in bliss eternally.

5 Farewell to all below the sun;
And as I pass in tears below,
The path is straight my feet shall run,
And God will keep me as I go;
And He will keep me in his hand,
And bring me to the promis'd land.

6 Farewell, farewell! I look above;
Jesus my friend, to thee I call;
My joy, my crown, my only love,
My safeguard here, my heavenly ALL.

My theme to preach, my song to sing,
My only hope till death—Amen.

223

7s.

DANIEL'S wisdom may I know,
Stephen's faith and patience show;
John's divine communion feel;
Moses' meekness, Joshua's zeal;
Run like the unwearied Paul,
Win the prize and conquer all.

2 Mary's love may I possess,
Lydia's tender-heartedness;
Peter's ardent spirit feel,
James' faith by works reveal:
Like young Timothy, may I
Every sinful passion fly.

3 Job's submission let me show,
David's true devotion know;
Samuel's call, O may I hear,
Lazarus' happy portion share;
Let Isaiah's hallow'd fire
All my new-born soul inspire.

4 Mine be Jacob's wrestling pray'r,
Gideon's valiant, steadfast care;
Joseph's purity impart,
Isaac's meditative heart,—
Abraham's friendship;—let me prove
Faithful to the God of love.

5 Most of all may I pursue
That example JESUS drew;

In my life and conduct show
How he liv'd and walk'd below;
Day by day, through grace bestow'd,
Imitate my dearest Lord.

6 Then shall I those worthies meet,
With them bow at Jesus' feet,
With them praise the God of love,
With them share the joys above:
With them range the blissful shore,
Meet them all to part no more.

224 8s. 7s. & 4s.

DAY of Judgment day of wonders!
Hark! the trumpet's awful sound,
Louder than a thousand thunders,
Shakes the vast creation round:
How the summons
Will the sinner's heart confound!

2 See the Judge, our nature wearing,
Clothed in majesty divine;
You, who long for his appearing,
Then shall say, "This God is mine:"
Gracious Savior,
Own me in that day for thine.

3 At his call the dead awaken,
Rise to life from earth and sea;
All the powers of nature, shaken
By his voice, prepare to flee:
Careless sinner,
What will then become of thee?

4 But to those who have confessed,
Loved and served the Lord below,
He will say, "Come near, ye blessed;
See the kingdom I bestow;
You forever
Shall my love and glory know."

225

8s. 7s. & 4s.

GENTLY, Lord, O, gently lead us
Through this lowly vale of tears;
And, O Lord, in mercy give us
Thy rich grace in all our fears:
O refresh us—
O refresh us with thy grace.

2 Though ten thousand ills beset us,
From without and from within,
Jesus says he'll ne'er forget us,
But will save from every sin:
Therefore praise him—
Praise the great Redeemer's name.

3 Though distresses now attend thee,
And thou tread'st the thorny road,
His right hand shall still defend thee—
Soon he'll bring thee home to God:
Therefore praise him—
Praise the great Redeemer's name.

4 O that I could now adore him
Like the heavenly host above,
Who forever bow before him,
And, unceasing, sing his love!

Happy songsters!
When shall I your chorus join?

226
12s. & 11s.

HOW painfully pleasing the fond recollection
Of youthful emotions and innocent joy,
When blest with paternal advice and affection,
Surrounded with mercies, with peace from on high!
I still view the chair of my father and mother,
The seats of their offspring as ranged on each hand,
And that richest book which excels every other,
The family Bible, which lay on the stand.
The old-fashioned Bible, the dear blessed Bible,
The family Bible, that lay on the stand.

2 That Bible, the volume of God's inspiration,
At morn and at evening could yield us delight;
The prayer of our sire was a sweet invocation
For mercy by day and for safety through night.
Our hymns of thanksgiving with harmony swelling,
All warm from the heart of a family band,
Half raised us from earth to that rapturous dwelling
Described in the Bible that lay on the stand.
The old-fashioned Bible, &c.

3 Ye scenes of tranquility, long have we parted,
My hopes almost gone, and my parents no more;
In sorrow and sadness I live broken-hearted,
And wander unknown on a far-distant shore.
Yet how can I doubt my Redeemer's protection,
Forgetful of gifts from his bountiful hand?
O, let me, with patience, receive his correction,
And think of the Bible that lay on the stand;
The old-fashioned Bible, &c.

227
C. P. M.

AWAKED by Sinai's awful sound,
My soul in guilt and thrall I found,

Exposed to endless wo;
Eternal truth did loud proclaim,
"The sinner must be born again,"
Or else to ruin go.

2 Amazed I stood, but could not tell
Which way to shun the gates of hell,
For death and hell drew near;
I strove, indeed, but strove in vain;
"The sinner must be born again"
Still sounded in my ear.

3 When to the law I trembling fled,
It poured its curses on my head;
I no relief could find.
This fearful truth increased my pain;
"The sinner must be born again"
O'erwhelmed my tortured mind.

4 Again did Sinai's thunder roll,
And guilt lay heavy on my soul,
A vast, oppressive load:
Alas! I read and saw it plain,
"The sinner must be born again,"
Or feel the wrath of God.

5 The saints I heard with rapture tell
How Jesus conquered death and hell,
And broke the fowler's snare;
Yet when I found this truth remain,
"The sinner must be born again,"
I sunk in deep despair.

6 But while I thus in anguish lay,
The gracious Savior passed this way,

And felt his pity move:
The sinner, by his justice slain,
Now by his grace is born again,
And sings redeeming love.

228 8s. & 6s.

JUST as I am without one plea,
But that thy blood was shed for me,
And that thou bid'st me come to thee,
O Lamb of God, I come!

2 Just as I am, and waiting not,
To rid my soul of one dark blot,
To thee whose blood can cleanse each spot,
O Lamb of God, I come!

3 Just as I am though tossed about
With many a conflict, many a doubt,
Fightings within, and fears without,
O Lamb of God, I come!

4 Just as I am—poor, wretched, blind;
Sight, riches, healing of the mind,
Yea, all I need in thee to find,
O Lamb of God, I come!

5 Just as I am, thou wilt receive,
Wilt welcome, pardon, cleanse, relieve;
Because thy promise, I believe,
O Lamb of God, I come!

6 Just as I am—thy love unknown
Has broken every barrier down;
Now, to be thine, yea, thine alone,
O Lamb of God, I come!

229

7s.

WHEN thy mortal life is fled,
When the death-shades o'er thee spread,
When is finished thy career,
Sinner, where wilt thou appear?

2 When the world has passed away,
When draws near the judgment day,
When the awful trump shall sound,
Say, O where wilt thou be found?

3 When the Judge descends in light,
Clothed in majesty and might,
When the wicked quail with fear,
Where, O, where wilt thou appear?

4 What shall soothe thy bursting heart,
When the saints and thou must part?
When the good with joy are crowned,
Sinner, where wilt thou be found?

5 While the Holy Ghost is nigh,
Quickly to the Savior fly;
Then shall peace thy spirit cheer;
Then in heaven shalt thou appear.

230

S. M.

HOW sweet the melting lay,
Which breaks upon the ear,
When at the hour of rising day,
Believers join in prayer!

2 The breezes waft their cries
Up to Jehovah's throne;
He listens to their humble sighs,
And sends his blessings down.

3 So Jesus rose to pray
Before the morning light,—
Once on the chilling mount did stay,
And wrestle all the night.

4 Glory to God on high,
Who sends his blessings down
To rescue souls condemned to die,
And make his people one.

231 L. M.

FROM every stormy wind that blows,
From every swelling tide of woes,
There is a calm, a sure retreat;
'T is found before the mercy-seat.

2 There is a place where Jesus sheds
The oil of gladness on our heads—
A place of all on earth most sweet;
It is the blood-bought mercy-seat.

3 There is a scene where spirits blend,
Where friend holds fellowship with friend;
Though sundered far, by faith they meet
Around one common mercy-seat.

4 There, there, on eagle wings we soar,
And sin and sense molest no more;
And heaven comes down our souls to greet,
And glory crowns the mercy-seat.

232 S. M.

HOW charming is the place
Where my Redeemer God
Unveils the beauties of his face,
And sheds his love abroad!

To him their prayers and cries
Each humble soul presents:
He listens to their broken sighs,
And grants them all their wants.

3 To them his sovereign will
He graciously imparts;
And in return accepts, with smiles,
The tribute of their hearts.

4 Give me, O Lord, a place
Within thy blest abode,
Among the children of thy grace,
The servants of my God.

233 7s.

FOR a season called to part,
Let us now ourselves commend
To the gracious eye and heart
Of our ever-present Friend.

2 Jesus, hear our humble prayer;
Tender Shepherd of thy sheep,
Let thy mercy and thy care
All our souls in safety keep.

3 In thy strength may we be strong;
Sweeten every cross and pain;
And our wasting lives prolong,
Till we meet on earth again.

234 L. M.

SOFT be the gently breathing notes,
That sing the Savior's dying love;
Soft as the evening zephyr floats,
Soft as the tuneful lyres above.
How blest the righteous when they die,
When holy souls retire to rest!
How mildly beams the closing eye!
How gently heaves th' expiring breast!

2 Soft as the morning dews descend,
While the sweet lark exulting soars;
So soft, to your Almighty Friend,
Be every sigh your bosom pours.
So fades a summer cloud away:
So sinks the gale when storms are o'er;
So gently shuts the eye of day:
So dies a wave along the shore.

3 True as the magnet to the pole,
So true let your contrition be—
So true let all your sorrows roll,
To him who bled upon the tree.
Farewell, conflicting hopes and fears,
Where lights and shades alternate dwell!
How bright th' unchanging morn appears!
Farewell, inconstant world, farewell.

235 C. M.

I SAW a wide and well-spread board,
  And children young and fair,
Come one by one, the eldest first,
  And took their stations there,
All neatly clad and beautiful,
  And with familiar tread,
They gathered round with joy to feast
  On meats and snow-white bread.

2 Beside the board the father sat,
  A smile his features wore
As on the little group he gazed,
  And told their portions o'er.
A meagre form arrayed in rags
  Anear the threshold stood,
A half-starved child had wandered there,
  To beg a little food.

3 Said one, "Why standest here, my dear?
  See, there's a vacant seat
Amid the children—and enough
  For them and thee to eat."
"Alas, for me!" the child replied,
  In tones of deep despair:
"No right have I amid your group,
  I have no father there."

4 Oh hour of fate! when from the skies
  With notes of deepest dread
The far resounding trump of God
  Shall summon forth the dead,

What countless hosts shall stand without
  The heavenly threshold fair,
And, gazing on the blest, exclaim
  I have no father there.

236 L. M.

KINDRED in Christ, for his dear sake
  A hearty welcome here receive;
May we together now partake
  The joys which only he can give.

2 May He, by whose kind care we meet,
  Send his good spirit from above,
Make our communications sweet,
  And cause our hearts to burn with love.

3 Forgotten be each worldly theme,
  When Christians see each other thus;
We only wish to speak of Him
  Who lived, and died, and reigns, for us.

4 Thus, as the moments pass away,
  We'll love, and wonder, and adore,
And long to see the glorious day
  When we shall meet to part no more.

237 S. M.

THE hours of evening close;
  Its lengthened shadows drawn
O'er scenes of earth, invite repose,
  And wait the Sabbath dawn.

2 So let its calm prevail
O'er forms of outward care,
Nor thought of earthly things assail
The still retreat of prayer.

3 Our guardian Shepherd near,
His watchful eye will keep,
And safe from violence or fear,
Will fold his flock to sleep.

4 So may a holier light
Than earth's our spirit rouse,
And call us, strengthened by his might,
To pay the Lord our vows.

238 L. M.

BEHOLD a stranger at the door!
He gently knocks—has knocked before;
Has waited long—is waiting still:
You treat no other friend so ill.

2 O, lovely Savior, see, he stands
With melting heart and loaded hands!
O, matchless kindness! and he shows
This matchless kindness to his foes.

3 But will he prove a friend indeed?
He will; the very friend you need:
The friend of sinners—yes, 'tis He,
With garments dyed on Calvary.

4 Admit him, ere his anger burn—
His feet departed ne'er return:
Admit him, or the hour's at hand
You'll at his door rejected stand.

239 C. M.

AMAZING grace,—how sweet the sound,
That saved a wretch like me!
I once was lost, but now am found;
Was blind, but now I see.

2 'T was grace that taught my heart to fear,
And grace my fears relieved;
How precious did that grace appear,
The hour I first believed!

3 Through many dangers, toils, and snares,
I have already come:
But grace has brought me safe thus far,
And grace will lead me home.

4 Yes, when this flesh and heart shall fail,
And mortal life shall cease,
I shall possess, within the veil,
A life of joy and peace.

240 C. M.

WHEN God revealed his gracious name,
And changed my mournful state,
My rapture seemed a pleasing dream,
The grace appeared so great.

2 The world beheld the glorious change,
And did thy hand confess;
My tongue broke out in unknown strains,
And sung surprising grace.

3 "Great is the work," my neighbors cried,
And owned thy power divine;

" Great is the work," my heart replied,
"And be the glory thine."

4 The Lord can clear the darkest skies,
Can give us day for night,
Make drops of sacred sorrow rise
To rivers of delight.

5 Let those who sow in sadness wait
Till the fair harvest come;
They shall confess their sheaves are great,
And shout the blessings home.

241 L. M.

O THOU my soul forget no more
The Friend who all thy sorrows bore;
Let every idol be forgot;
But O my soul forget him not.

2 Renounce thy works and ways, with grief,
And fly to this divine relief;
Nor Him forget, who left his throne,
And for thy life gave up his own.

3 Eternal truth and mercy shine
In him, and he himself is thine:
And canst thou, then, with sin beset,
Such charms, such matchless charms, forget?

4 O, no; till life itself depart,
His name shall cheer and warm my heart;
And, lisping this, from earth I'll rise,
And join the chorus of the skies.

242

L. M.

LIFE is the time to serve the Lord,
The time t' insure the great reward;
And while the lamp holds out to burn,
The vilest sinner may return.

2 Life is the hour that God hath given
To 'scape from hell and fly to heaven—
The day of grace; and mortals may
Secure the blessings of the day.

3 Then what my thoughts design to do,
My hands with all your might pursue,
Since no device, nor work, is found,
Nor faith, nor hope, beneath the ground.

243

The Dying Girl.

"GO bring them," said the dying fair,
With anguish in her tone:
"Those spotless robes, and jewels rare,
Go bring them every one."
They strewed them on her dying bed,
Those robes of princely cut;
"Father," with bitterness she said,
"For these my soul is lost."

2 "With glorious hopes I once was bless'd,
Nor feared the gaping tomb:
With heaven already in my breast,
I looked for heaven to come

I heard a Savior's pardoning voice,
  My soul was fill'd with peace;
Father, you bought me with mere toys,
  I bartered heaven for these."

3 "Take them, they are the price of blood,
  For these I've lost my soul,
For these, must bear the wrath of God,
  While endless ages roll.
Remember when you look on these,
  Your daughter's fearful doom,
That she, her pride and thine to please,
  Went wailing to the tomb."

4 "Come, take them from my sight and touch,
  Your gifts I now restore:
Keep them with care, they cost you much,
  They cost your daughter more.
"Look on them every rolling year,
  On this my dying day,
And shed for me the burning tear,"
  She said—*and sank away.*

244 C. M.

GOD moves in a mysterious way,
  His wonders to perform;
He plants his footsteps in the sea,
  And rides upon the storm.

2 Deep in unfathomable mines
  Of never-failing skill,
He treasures up his bright designs,
  And works his sov'reign will.

3 Ye fearful saints, fresh courage take;
The clouds ye so much dread
Are big with mercy, and shall break
In blessings on your head.

4 Judge not the Lord by feeble sense,
But trust him for his grace;
Behind a frowning providence
He hides a smiling face!

5 His purposes will ripen fast,
Unfolding every hour;
The bud may have a bitter taste,
But sweet will be the flower.

6 Blind unbelief is sure to err,
And scan his work in vain;
God is his own interpreter;
And he will make it plain.

245 C. M.

WHILE shepherds watched their flocks by night,
All seated on the ground,
The angel of the Lord came down,
And glory shone around.

2 Fear not, said he, (for mighty dread
Had seized their troubled mind,)
Glad tidings of great joy I bring,
To you and all mankind.

3 To you, in David's town, this day
Is born, of David's line,

The Savior, who is Christ the Lord;
And this shall be the sign:

4 The heavenly babe you there shall find
To human view display'd,
All meanly wrapped in swathing-bands,
And in a manger laid.

5 Thus spake the seraph: and forthwith
Appear'd a shining throng
Of angels, praising God on high,
Who thus address'd their song:

6 All glory be to God on high,
And to the earth be peace:
Good-will henceforth, from heaven to men,
Begin and never cease.

246

AIR—"*Funeral Bell.*"

FAR, far o'er hill and dell,
On the winds stealing
List to the tolling bell,
Mournfully pealing;
Hark! hark! it seems to say,
As melt those sounds away,
So earthly joys decay,
Whilst new their feeling.

2 Now through the charmed air,
On the winds stealing,
List to the mourner's prayer,
Solemnly bending:
Hark! hark! it seems to say,
Turn from those joys away

To those which ne'er decay,
  For life is ending.

3 O'er a father's dismal tomb,
  See the orphan bending,
From the solemn church-yard's gloom
  Hear the dirge ascending:
Hark! hark! it seems to say,
  How short ambition's sway,
Life's joys and friendship's ray
  In the dark grave ending.

4 So when our mortal ties,
  Death shall dissever,
Lord, may we reach the skies,
  Where care comes never;
And in eternal day,
  Joining the angel's lay,
To our Creator pay
  Homage forever.

SABBATH SCHOOL HYMNS.

247

7s. & 8s.

WHEN our Fathers, long ago,
  Fled from persecution's flame,
O'er the dark tempestuous sea,
  Little children with them came.
Little children knelt and pray'd,
  With their Sires on freedom's shore,
Rais'd the grateful notes of joy,
  Louder than the ocean's roar.

2 Bursting on night's darkest hour,
  Children heard the savage yell,
And the loud and fearful cry,
  Of their parents, as they fell.
Children sang in later times,
  Liberty's inspiring lay,
Glowing hearts in concert hailed,
  Each returning festal day.

3 But a nobler, sweeter song,
  We this day have met to sing,
Praise to him in Bethlehem born,
  Him, our Savior and our King.
He has conquered—lo he comes,
  Leading captive death and sin;
Open, open wide your gates,
  Let the King of glory in.

4 Jesus, Jesus, yes! 't is he,
  Evermore the children's friend,

We have one request for thee,
Teachers, faithful teachers send,
Send them through this guilty world,
To make glad th' abodes of sin,
Open, open wide your gates,
Let the King of glory in.

248 7s.

HOLY Father, please to hear,
Children's praise and humble prayer,
Thou didst give us parents kind,
Teach us ever them to mind.

2 Food and raiment, home and friends,
All we have, thy goodness sends,
And for these, our hearts shall raise
Grateful thanks, and humble praise.

3 Guide our lives in grace and truth,
Through the tempting scene of youth,
And when here our trials cease,
O receive our souls in peace.

249 S. M.

OURS is the Sabbath school,
Its lessons may we prize,
And grow by every gospel rule,
Unto salvation wise.

2 So all our lives below,
In wisdom's pleasant ways,
The fruits of Sabbath schools shall show
The bliss of Sabbath days.

3 Then heaven itself shall be,
Our Sabbath school above,
And undisturbed eternity,
One Sabbath school of love.

250 H. M.

HOW kind the Savior's love,
How tenderly he smiled,
While in his arms he took
And blest each little child.
Forbid them not, for such I came,
I love to hear them lisp my name.

2 How oft our teachers pray,
Their efforts do not cease,
That we may find the way,
To happiness and peace.
Urge the message he has sent,
Entreating children to repent.

ANTI-SLAVERY HYMNS.

251 8s. & 7s.
AIR—"*Mount Vernon.*"

HEARKEN, Christian, hear the groaning
Of the poor oppressed slave;
Hear him now his state bemoaning;
None to pity, none to save.

2 Listen friends of every nation,
To the wailing bondman's plea,
Hear his doleful lamentation,
Hear him sigh for liberty.

3 See him writhe in dreadful anguish,
On his back the stripes are laid;
Can you see him pine and languish,
And refuse to lend him aid?

4 Will you by your votes and silence
Servitude perpetuate?
Can you look without abhorrence
On a system God doth hate?

5 Can you bow with cold indifference,
And the throne of God address?
Will you there ask no assistance
For the bondman in distress?

6 Think ye sons of ease and freedom,
Of the suff'rings he endures;
You would sigh for liberation,
Were the slave's condition yours.

7 Waken from your sinful slumber,
Shake off now your lethargy,
Burst oppression's chains asunder,
Set the willing captive free.

8 To the contest—onward, freemen,
Sound aloud the jubilee;
To the rescue, sons of freedom,
Give the slave his liberty.

252

8s. 7s. & 4s.
AIR—"*Zion.*"

HARK! a voice from heaven proclaiming,
Comfort to the mourning slave;
God has heard him long complaining,
And extends his arm to save;
Proud oppression,
Soon shall find a shameful grave, &c.

2 See the light of truth is breaking,
Full and clear on every hand:
And the voice of mercy speaking,
Now is heard through all the land.
Firm and fearless,
See the friends of freedom stand, &c.

3 Lo! the nation is arousing
From its slumber long and deep;
And the friends of God are waking,
Never, never more to sleep,
While a bondman
In his chains remains to weep, &c.

4 Long, too long, have we been dreaming
O'er our country's sin and shame.

Let us now, the time redeeming,
  Press the helpless captive's claim,
    Till, exulting,
  He shall cast aside his chain, &c.

253

C. M.
AIR—" *Ortonville.*

WHAT mean ye, that ye bruise and bind
  My people, saith the Lord,
And starve your craving brethren's mind
  Who ask to read my word?

2 What mean ye that ye make them toil,
  Through long and weary years;
And shed like rain upon your soil,
  Their blood and bitter tears?

3 What mean ye, when God's bounteous hand
  To you so much has given,
That from the slave who tills your land,
  You keep both earth and heaven?

4 What mean ye that ye dare to rend
  The tender mother's heart;
Brother from sister, friend from friend,
  How dare you make them part?

5 When at the judgment God shall call,
  Where is thy brother? say
What mean ye, to the Judge of all,
  To answer on that day?

254

L. M.
AIR—" *Old Hundred.*"

WE ask not that the slave should lie,
  As lies his master at his ease,

Beneath a silken canopy,
  Or in the shade of blooming trees.

2 We mourn not that the man should toil;
  'T is nature's need, 't is God's decree;
But let the hand that tills the soil,
  Be, like the wind that fans it, free.

3 We ask not, 'eye for eye,' that all,
  Who forge the chain and ply the whip,
Should feel their torture; while the thrall
  Should wield the scourge of mastership.

4 We only ask, O God, that they
  Who bind a brother, may relent:
But, Great Avenger, we do pray
  That the wrong-doer may repent.

255

L. M.
AIR—"*Wells.*"

THE hour of freedom! come it must—
  O, hasten it in mercy, Heaven!
When all, who grovel in the dust,
  Shall stand erect, their fetters riven.

2 When glorious freedom shall be won
  By every caste, complexion, clime,
When tyranny shall be o'erthrown,
  And color cease to be a crime.

3 Friend of the poor, long-suff'ring Lord!
  This guilty land from ruin save;
Let justice sheathe her glitt'ring sword,
  And mercy rescue from the grave.

4 And ye, who are like cattle sold,
Ignobly trodden like the earth,
And barter'd constantly for gold,
Your souls debased from their high birth,

5 Bear meekly still your cruel woes,
Light follows darkness, comfort, pain;
So time shall give you sweet repose,
And sever ev'ry hateful chain.

256

8s. & 7s.
AIR—*Zion.*

SEE yon glorious star ascending
Brightly o'er the Southern sea;
Truth and peace to earth portending,
Herald of a Jubilee.
Hail it, Freemen,
'T is the star of Liberty.

2 Dim at first, but widely spreading,
Soon 't will burst supremely bright;
Life and health and comfort shedding,
O'er the shades of moral night.
Hail it, Bondmen,
Slavery cannot bear its light.

3 Few its rays—'t is but the dawning
Of the reign of truth and peace;
Joy to slaves, yet sad forewarning
To the tyrants of our race.
Tremble Tyrants,
Soon your cruel power will cease.

4 Earth is brighten'd by the glory
Of its mild and peaceful rays;
Ransom'd slaves shall tell the story,
See its light, and sing its praise.
Hail it, Christians,
Harbinger of better days.

257

6s. & 4s.
AIR—"*America.*"

MY country! 't is of thee,
Strong hold of slavery,
Of thee I sing:
Land where my fathers died,
Where men man's rights deride,
From every mountain side,
Thy deeds shall ring.

2 My native country! thee,
Where all men are born free,
If white their skin:
I love thy hills and dales,
Thy mounts and pleasant vales,
But hate thy negro sales,
As foulest sin.

3 Let wailing swell the breeze,
And ring from all the trees,
The black man's wrong;
Let every tongue awake,
Let bond and free partake,
Let rocks their silence break,
The sound prolong.

4 Our Father's God! to thee,
Author of liberty,

To thee we sing;
Soon may our land be bright,
With holy freedom's right,
Protect us by thy might,
Great God, our King.

258 AIR—*Araby's Daughter.*

THE slave-mother leaned on her mattock full weary,*
At the grey of the dawn, in that home of the dead;
Where the tall city's shade made each green grave look dreary,
Though spangled with tears which kind nature had shed.
But she recked not that cold dews were falling around her,
Though weary with toil, and though fainting for food,
For the last tie was broke which to feeling had bound her,
And froze e'en the fondness for life in her blood.

2 Her children as mothers love, once she had loved them:
But sold were they all save the corpse by her side:
God saw all her fears for her child, and removed them;
And her last pulse of hope with her last babe had died.

---

* In the year 1844, near the city of Louisville, Ky., as the sexton went to open a grave-yard, he found there a slave mother digging a grave for her own infant, which, without shroud or coffin, was lying by her on the earth. Her mistress had sent her thus to bury her infant, to save the expense of grave-clothes and coffin!"

O, then, though she knew its young eyes first met her,
In language of smiles which the lips could not speak,
She thought that its safety in death was far better,
Than the joy she had felt when it breathed on her cheek.

3 And she prayed, as she turned to her strange task, preparing
The shroudless and coffinless rest for her child,
That soon her torn breast might her babe's sleep be sharing,
Her heart no more rung, and her brain no more wild:
For she said, while around her damp vapors aspirant,
Rose chill from the moist turf which covered the grave,
That earth was less cold than the heart of a tyrant,
And death far less drear than the life of a slave.

259

S. M.
AIR—" *Laban.*"

HOW long shall Afric's sons,
Be sons of grief and pain,
How long shall slavery curse the earth,
And mercy plead in vain ?

2 Lift up your voice to-day
In Freedom's holy cause,
Till all the world in love obey
Their Maker's righteous laws.

3 Then in your blissful songs,
Shall bond and free unite,
His praise to spread, to whom belongs
All majesty and might.

260 7s.
AIR—*Pleyel's Hymn.*

LORD deliver; thou canst save;
Save from evil, Mighty God;
Hear, oh, hear the kneeling slave,
Break, oh break the oppressor's rod.

2 May the captive's pleading fill
All the earth and all the sky;
Every other voice be still,
While he pleads with God on high.

3 He, whose ear is every where,
Who doth silent sorrow see,
Will regard the captive's prayer,
Will from bondage set him free.

4 Love to man and love to God,
Are the weapons of our war;
These can break th' oppressor's rod,
Burst the bonds that we abhor.

261 7s. & 6s.
AIR—*Morning light is breaking.*

SOON shall the trump of Freedom,
Resound from shore to shore;
Soon taught by heavenly wisdom,
Man shall oppress no more;
But ev'ry yoke be broken,
Each captive soul set free,
And every heart shall welcome
The day of Jubilee.

2 Then tyrants' crowns and sceptres,
And victors' wreaths and cars;
And galling chains and fetters,
With all the pomp of wars,
Shall in the dust be trodden,
Till time shall be no more;
And peace and joy from heaven
The Lord on earth shall pour.

262

7s. & 6s.
AIR—"*Scots wha hae.*"

CHILDREN of the glorious dead,
Who for freedom fought and bled,
With her banner o'er you spread,
On to victory;
Not for stern ambition's prize,
Let your hopes or wishes rise,
Lo! your leader from the skies,
Bids you do or die.

2 This is proud oppression's hour,
Storms assail you, will you cow'r,
While beneath a despot's power,
Groans the suff'ring slave,
While on ev'ry southern gale,
Comes the helpless captive's tale,
Comes a voice of woman's wail,
And of man's despair?

3 Never! by your country's shame,
Never! by a Savior's claim,
To the men of ev'ry name,
Whom he died to save;
Onward, then, ye fearless band,
Heart to heart, and hand to hand;

Yours shall be the Christian's stand,
Or the martyr's grave.

263

TUNE—"*Oft in the stilly night.*"

OFT in the chilly night,
Ere slumber's chain has bound me,
When all her silvery light
The moon is pouring round me,
Beneath the ray,
I kneel and pray
That God would give some token,
That slavery's chains,
On Southern plains,
Shall all ere long be broken.
Yes, in the chilly night,
Though slavery's chain has bound me,
Kneel I, and feel the might
Of God's right arm around me.

2 When at the driver's call,
In cold or sultry weather,
We slaves, both great and small,
Turn out to toil together,
I feel like one,
From whom the sun
Of hope has long departed;
And morning's light,
And weary night
Still find me broken-hearted.
Thus, when the chilly breath
Of night is sighing round me,
Kneel I, and wish that death
In his cold chain had bound me.

TEMPERANCE HYMNS.

264 C. M.
AIR—" *Ortonville.*"

MY mind to me a kingdom is,
 And I would have it free;
For though its small in glory's eyes,
 'T is all the world to me.

2 It roves about and sweetly brings,
 From earth, and sea, and sky,
Ten thousand bright and glorious things,
 Unseen by mortal eye.

3 O! let it once be quench'd and mute,
 And lose its eagle ken;
Then I should sink below the brute,
 That shuns the haunts of men.

4 There's scarce a brute that God has made,
 That would not master me;
Or all my strength, without its aid,
 Would its own murderer be.

5 The drunkard's drowsy powers alas!
 How weak, and faint, and dim!
Like spectral shades they flit and pass,—
 What are they worth to him?

6 They change the peaceful joys of home,
 To deadliest hate and wo,
And throw a sombre robe of gloom,
 On loveliest scenes below.

7 His lively babes that climb his knee,
And laugh his welcome home,
Insulting brats appear to be,
That mock to see him come;

8 And she who meets him at the door,
And smiles her grief to hide,
E'en she, he thinks insults him more,
Than all the world beside.

9 If I the drunkard's bowl reject,
And never taste a jot,
Shall I command the less respect,
Than yonder trembling sot?

10 O! may my mind be not like his,
Then I can sing with glee,
'My mind to me a kingdom is,'
'T is all the world to me.

265

AIR—"*Sweet Home.*"

MID sorrows and sadness I'm destined to roam,
Forlorn, and forsaken, deprived of my home;
Intemperance hath robbed me of all that was dear,
Of my home in the skies, and my happiness here.
"Home! home! sweet, sweet home!"
An exile from God, I shall ne'er find a home.

2 I vainly presumed when I first took the cup,
I could drink if I chose, or I could give it up;
But I tampered too long, too long tempted Heaven,
Till an outcast from God, and his presence I'm driven.
"Home! home! sweet, sweet home!"
On earth or in heaven, I shall ne'er find a home.

3 My heart-broken wife in her grave hath found rest,
And my children have gone to the land of the blest;
While I a poor wretch, a vile wanderer like Cain,
With the "mark" of the beast, on the earth still remain.
"Home! home! sweet, sweet home!"
How happy was I with my loved ones at home.

4 Farewell to the social endearments of home;
Justly loathed by my fellows I wander alone;
For presumptuously sinning and tempting the Lord,
Of the fruit of my ways I must reap the reward.
"Home! home! sweet, sweet home!"
An exile from God, I shall ne'er find a home.

266

C. M.
AIR—"*Auld Lang Syne.*"

WITH banner and with badge we come,
An army true and strong,
To fight against the hosts of Rum,
And this shall be our song:

CHORUS.

We love the clear Cold Water Springs,
Supplied by gentle showers;
We feel the strength cold water brings,
"The victory is ours."

2 Cold Water-Army is our name,
O may we faithful be,
And so, in truth and justice claim
The blessings of the free.
We love the clear Cold Water Springs, &c.

3 Though others love their rum and wine,
And drink till they are mad,
To water we will still incline,

To make us strong and glad.
We love the clear Cold Water Springs, &c.

4 I pledge to thee this hand of mine,
In faith and friendship strong:
And fellow-soldiers we will join
The chorus of our song.
We love the clear Cold Water Springs, &c.

267 Air—"*Araby's Daughter.*"

HARK! hark ye, O listen to the sorrow and weeping,
Which rise from the hovel where misery reigns;
To the howl of the winds a wild harmony keeping,
Which chills the warm life-blood that speeds thro' our veins!
Sad, sad is the story those accents are telling,
Like the wail of the dying it pierces the air;
Oh, what has so blasted that comfortless dwelling?
The monster intemperance is rioting there!

2 The wife, worse than widowed, forlorn and heart-broken,
While hunger and want make her little ones cry,
All trembling and pale, hears her terrible token
Of anguish, the steps of her husband are nigh!
Those sounds she once caught with unspeakable gladness,
While lit with affection her eye brightly shone,
Now sink on her bosom, o'er burdened with sadness,
Like the funeral knell, or the dirge's low moan!

3 He comes! see, he comes! but no fond salutation,
Breaks forth from his lips which once murmured of love;
Those eyes once accustomed to smile approbation,
Look dark as the storm-cloud which mutters above!

With oaths and reproaches he vents his displeasure,
And smites the frail form he has vowed to protect;
Her tears and entreaties avail in no measure,—
He treats them with scorn, or with cruel neglect.

4 His babes who once crowded around for his blessing,
And sat gaily prattling for joy on his knee;
Familiar with blows in the place of caressing,
Away from their father instinctively flee!
Oh! the withering curse and the ruin appalling,
Which Alcohol wreaks on a suffering world!
Let the people's rebuke like hot thunderbolts falling,
Shower fierce on the fiend, till from earth he is hurled!

268

AIR—"*The rose that all are praising.*

THE drink that's in the drunkard's bowl,
Is not the drink for me;
It kills his body and his soul;
How sad a sight is he!
But there's a drink which God hath given,
Distilling in the showers of heaven,
In measures large and free;
O, that's the drink for me,
O, that's the drink for me,
O, that's the drink for me.

2 The stream that many prize so high,
Is not the stream for me;
For he who drinks it, still is dry,
And ever dry he'll be.
But there's a stream so cool and clear,
The thirsty traveller lingers near,

Refreshed and glad is he;
O, that's the stream for me,
O, that's the stream for me,
O, that's the stream for me.

3 The wine cup that so many prize,
Is not the cup for me.
The aching head, the bloated face,
In its sad train I see.
But there's a cup of water pure,
And he who drinks it may be sure,
Of health and length of days;
O, that's the cup for me,
O, that's the cup for me,
O, that's the cup for me.

269

AIR—"*Scots wha hae.*"

FRIENDS of Freedom swell the song,
Young and old the strain prolong,
Make the temp'rance army strong,
And on to victory:
Lift your banners, let them wave,
Onward march a world to save,
Who would fill a drunkard's grave,
And bear his infamy?

2 Shrink not when the foe appears;
Spurn the coward's guilty fears,
Hear the shrieks, behold the tears,
Of ruined families.
Raise the cry in every spot,
'*Touch not*, *Taste not*, *Handle not*,'

Who would be a drunken sot,
The worst of miseries !

3 Give the aching bosom rest,
Carry joy to every breast,
Make the wretched drunkard blest,
By living soberly.
Raise the glorious watchword high,
'*Touch not, taste not, till you die,*'
Let the echo reach the sky,
And earth keep jubilee.

4 God of mercy hear us plead,
For thy help we intercede,
See how many bosoms bleed,
And heal them speedily.
Hasten, Lord, the happy day,
When, beneath thy gentle sway,
TEMPERANCE all the world shall sway,
And reign triumphantly.

INDEX OF FIRST LINES.

www.ingramcontent.com/pod-product-compliance
Lightning Source LLC
LaVergne TN
LVHW010251110826
845151LV00004B/1442
9781425522391